TO:

....

FROM:

....

100
devotions
for the
WORKING MOM

ZONDERVAN®

ZONDERVAN

100 Devotions for the Working Mom

Copyright © 2023 Zondervan

Requests for information should be addressed to:

Zondervan, *3900 Sparks Dr. SE, Grand Rapids, Michigan 49546*

Zondervan titles may be purchased in bulk for educational, business, fundraising, or sales promotional use. For information, please email SpecialMarkets@Zondervan.com.

ISBN 978-0-310-14081-8 (softcover)
ISBN 978-0-310-14083-2 (audio)
ISBN 978-0-310-14082-5 (ebook)

Cover design: Jamie DeBruyn

Interior design: Kristy Edwards

Printed in the United States of America
23 24 25 26 27 LBC 5 4 3 2 1

✤✤✤✤ *Introduction* ✤✤✤✤

*P*eace. As a working mom, what happens when you hear that word? Do you immediately sink into your chair, breathe deeply, and let go? Or does your heart cry out in longing? Does your body crave a reprieve from the hustle and bustle of your long days?

Finding peace in the midst of juggling a life of family and work can be difficult. Being pulled in a variety of directions on a daily basis can be demanding, overwhelming, and exhausting. In between deadlines at work, shifting schedules, cultivating marriage, young children, busy teens, elderly parents, friends, and bills that need to be paid, it can be challenging to find time with God. We run to and from meetings and obligations, scarfing down a hurried dinner. We say yes to building Legos, braiding hair, teaching teens how to drive, and laundry but often neglect to take a warm bath, settle into prayer, or take a few hours to let God minister to our souls. As we collapse on the couch at the end of the day, sometimes we seek nothing more than a way to numb our tired, aching brains. Does this sound familiar?

There is good news. There is hope. There is peace to be received, cultivated, and nourished. God is longing to meet with you. Yes, you!

If you're searching for a way to find balance as a working mom—if you're looking to satisfy the deep, God-given yearning in your soul and to quiet the buzzing in your mind that comes from too much activity and not enough downtime—this devotional is for you.

Jesus spoke candidly about the topic of peace. He knew that mothers would struggle over and over to find balance. That's why we can take comfort in His words in John 14:27: "Peace I leave with you; my peace I give to you. Not as the world gives do I give to you. Let not your hearts be troubled, neither let them be afraid" (ESV). Doesn't that sound wonderful? Jesus speaks truth and rest into our hearts.

These daily devotions are set up to remind you that you're not alone. Each day you'll read a Scripture verse, a devotional, and prayer. Use the ruled lines however you'd like—write down prayers, reflect and write down what's on your mind, make a list of goals, create affirmations, or simply journal about your feelings.

May you find hope in Him. May you breathe deeply. May you grasp the life-changing importance of stillness. May it overflow into your spouse, your children, and your extended family. May it encourage and strengthen your colleagues and work. May you know your importance and your worth in God as He calls you daily to a life in Him.

Day 1

Jesus often withdrew to lonely places and prayed.

LUKE 5:16

Peace doesn't just fall into your lap, and it won't tap you on your shoulder during a busy day. Rest, more often than not, must be sought out, especially for working mothers. It needs to be carved into each day, week, and month, and it needs to be intentional.

Think about your daily schedule. Do you have a slot specifically to take some time for yourself? You make time for picking up the kids, working, making dinner, or cleaning up the house, but is serenity a foreign concept?

Today's culture is busy. Your work life is busy. But that doesn't mean you cannot rest; it just needs to be added to your calendar. Just as you make time to see friends or go on a weekend getaway, time with God needs to be scheduled. Try getting up fifteen minutes earlier to sit in the quiet. Instead of browsing social media, take a walk outside and breathe deeply. Seek His peace, and you will be rewarded—mind, body, and soul. You will also find more joy in your work.

....

Lord, help me set aside time each day for peace among work, even when it seems impossible. You are the Giver of time, and You know how to balance my days. Remind me to meet with You, and You will take care of the rest.

....

....

....

....

....

....

....

....

....

....

....

....

....

....

....

....

....

....

....

Day 2

You gave abundant showers, O God; you
refreshed your weary inheritance.

Psalm 68:9

Is your heart downcast? Do you feel troubled? It's a common way to feel these days. This world has so much heartache. Our families carry wounds, friends let us down, loved ones pass away, careers are full of demands, and it may seem as if life is too hard to handle. We live in a broken world. And we live among broken people.

Perhaps today you are trying your best to fight against despair, but your prayers feel heavy. The weight of this struggle is dragging you down—and you're not sure if you have enough strength to get back up. You feel tired and discouraged with how much work there is on your plate.

Take heart, for the Lord will rescue you. You can let those burdens slide off your back; He promises to carry your heartache, your shame, and your sorrows. In the middle of this storm, remember that God promises to never leave or forsake you—and He means it. Find rest, in every circumstance, in Christ alone.

....

Lord, I'm no match for this life's trials and all the work to be done. Please give me comfort. Convict me in areas I need to change, and show me how to create proper boundaries while also lending a hand.

....

....

....

....

....

....

....

....

....

....

....

....

....

....

....

....

....

....

....

....

....

....

"Consider the ravens: They do not sow or reap, they have no storeroom or barn; yet God feeds them. And how much more valuable you are than birds!"

LUKE 12:24

The workday is over and the bills are coming in. Some are perhaps bigger than you were expecting for the month, and as you read them, your spirit begins to deflate. The soaring gas bill reflects your home's warmth during frigid temperatures, the credit card bill reminds you that the promotion you wanted fell through, and the repair bill to fix your car is cringe-worthy.

Are you worrying about finances? Is your neck knotting with stress? Remember, the Lord wants you to give Him every burden and every concern—from the biggest to the smallest. Today, confess your worry to Him. He is the ultimate Provider, and He promises to take care of His children. Take a deep breath and remember that God wants you to be free from worry, even if your bank account looks bleak. Trust in Him to provide for you as you are faithful to the job He's given you to do.

God, I put my trust in You, the Provider of all good things. You will not desert me. I will speak of Your faithfulness, and I will believe in Your goodness.

....

....

....

....

....

....

....

....

....

....

....

....

....

....

....

....

....

....

....

....

"I will refresh the weary and satisfy the faint."
JEREMIAH 31:25

When your alarm goes off on Monday, you may be tempted to hit Snooze. It can't be the workweek already, can it? Even if you love your job, starting a new week is sometimes difficult, especially if you've had a busy weekend.

While you can't go back and relive your weekend in a more restful manner, you can ensure that your week begins well. Today, instead of getting lunch with your colleagues, maybe you can drive to the park and eat in solitude. If your toddler watches an evening TV show, skip cleaning the kitchen and spend a few minutes in prayer. Refreshment can be found in the tiny opportunities throughout your day, and those moments can add up. Look for opportunities to find peace, soak them up, and use your time well. Self-care is available in this day—you just need to look for it.

....

Lord, refresh my spirit and open my eyes to opportunities to simply be. May I use my time in ways that honor You. Teach me how diligence and contentment can go hand in hand.

Be still before the Lord and wait patiently for him.

PSALM 37:7

There is nothing you can do to make God love you more—or less. Many people feel they must earn God's love. They think the more they perform at work, in their church, in their community, or at home, the more God will love them. But that isn't true, and if you're not careful, overworking can let exhaustion creep in and take over.

Careers, church, and service to others—all those things are good, but they won't make God's love for you grow. Be realistic with yourself and your limits. If you have the time and energy to take on a promotion, then by all means, do it. But if the thought of one more thing makes you want to cry, don't feel any guilt or shame. You cannot earn God's love by being busier. The best things you can do for your relationship with Him are to sit in His presence, study His Word, and talk with Him. Rest in that truth today.

....

Thank You, Father, for Your unshakable and unchangeable love. Fill me afresh with reminders of Your love for me so that I can follow You well. Open my eyes to how You want to minister to me today.

....

....

....

....

....

....

....

....

....

....

....

....

....

....

....

....

....

....

....

....

....

....

What do people get for all the toil and anxious
striving with which they labor under the sun?
ECCLESIASTES 2:22

Social media can be fun, but it also can be harmful. If you find yourself trying to match your life to what you see online, your efforts will be futile. Whether it's on Facebook or Instagram, TikTok or Twitter, these are only snapshots and sound bites of another's life. Everyone has different circumstances, and you don't know what theirs are. The reality is, no one is posting their mess.

If you're trying to make your life look picture-perfect, take a break. Instead of seeing yourself through the lens of someone else's camera, experience your life. It may be messy, broken, and full of deadlines. But there are also moments that make you laugh out loud and shout with joy, holy moments that remain ingrained in your mind forever. It's your life, your family, and your occupation—all in its glorious imperfection. Life doesn't need to be photo-worthy to be worth a great deal. Walk away from the pressure of a picture-perfect life and find grace. You'll be glad you did.

....

Remind me, Jesus, that this life really is about loving and pleasing You only, in my current circumstances. Help me learn contentment in imperfection, receiving each day as a gift. Help me to let go of unhealthy expectations and be met by Your mercy.

A generous person will prosper; whoever
refreshes others will be refreshed.

PROVERBS 11:25

D o you have colleagues or friends you are constantly trying to impress? Are any friendships in your life based on performance and appearance rather than true acceptance? If so, read these words: *they are not true friends.* Friendships should feel like a safe place to bare your heart and not a competition or audition. If yours don't allow you to let your guard down and confess your flaws, and if they don't bring you encouragement, then they may not be the type of friendships you need in your life.

You shouldn't need to strive for acceptance in friendships, nor in work relationships. Kindness does take intentionality, but you don't need to prove yourself time and time again. True friends care for you as you are. True friends allow your heart and mind to feel safe and valued. Especially as a working mother, it's important to have an inner circle who can uplift and care for you well.

Today, think of people in your life who provide you with true friendship, and thank the Lord for bringing them into your life.

....

Thank You, Lord, for blessing me with true relationships. May I never take them for granted. Show me opportunities to pray for, encourage, and uplift my friends. Help me to receive their gifts of support with humility as well.

God is not a God of disorder but of peace.
I Corinthians 14:33

*N*o. The word is only two letters long, but it is very difficult to say. Saying no could mean missing out on experiences, promotions, fun evenings out, or even traveling for work and pleasure. Saying no has a negative connotation—perhaps because it's so hard to hear that word ourselves.

Saying yes is much easier. It makes others happy. It lightens someone else's load, gets you a promotion, and makes you look like a better person. But sometimes the best answer is not yes.

In your search for peace, practice saying no. When your plate is too full and your brain is going in a million different directions, it's probably time to say no. You will find space to breathe and time to live your life instead of just getting through, day by day. And it will get easier. Saying no is actually saying yes to the people and things most important to you.

....

Lord, help me discern when to say yes and when to say no. Teach me how to value myself and my time by giving me proper parameters for my life. Give me confidence to make good decisions and stick to them.

"The LORD make his face shine on you and be gracious to you;
the LORD turn his face toward you and give you peace."

NUMBERS 6:25–26

We are our own worst critics. When you mess up during a work presentation, yell at your children, or put your foot in your mouth, you're often the one beating yourself up again and again. Dear friend, give yourself grace—the same grace you extend to other working moms.

You don't need to keep replaying your mistakes or reliving your bad moments. You can find comfort in the Savior who washes you clean, over and over. He does not hold any resentment toward you, and you can breathe deeply knowing that you are loved—flaws and all. So revel in the fact that you are covered with grace. And when you begin chastising yourself, when those words of self-condemnation ring in your ears, try to see yourself through the eyes of your loving Father.

Give yourself grace, and rest in the knowledge that He removes all your sins from you gladly and willingly.

....

Lord, Your forgiveness knows no bounds. Teach me to give myself grace.
Remind me that I am a human and perfectionism is not a present reality.
Mold me in Your love so that I can receive Your gift of peace.

....

....

....

....

....

....

....

....

....

....

....

....

....

....

....

....

....

....

He gives strength to the weary and increases the power of the weak.

ISAIAH 40:29

I'm so busy! How often have you uttered those words in the past year, month, week, or even day? Some wear busyness as a badge of honor, while others wear it as a burden. Either way, we need balance—whether it's easy to admit or not.

Why not try to have a mindset of peace instead of busyness? When your personal and work calendars are filling up with obligations, it can be easy to try to cram as much as possible into your week. Instead, ask yourself what would be most life-giving to you and your family. If the thought of serving on one more board, or hosting one more party, or squeezing in one more meeting leaves you feeling deflated, then say no.

Choose a mindset of contentment. It's okay to be selective about what you add to your calendar. Let God frame your week instead of busyness. It will greatly impact your mental health and attitude.

....

Lord, remind me to have a mindset of balance today and throughout this workweek. You don't want me frazzled and overwhelmed. You want me filled to overflowing. Grant me the grace to accept Your power in the midst of my weakness.

....

....

....

....

....

....

....

....

....

....

....

....

....

....

....

....

....

....

....

....

....

A heart at peace gives life to the body.

PROVERBS 14:30

W hat brings you life and makes you smile outside of work? Is it a weekend spent camping under the stars? Is it kneading dough and watching it rise? Maybe it's writing or playing music. These things that make you smile are important to living a full life. If your days are simply spent working, sleeping, and paying the bills, it's time for a change. It's time to focus on you—not because the world revolves around you but because we all need to practice self-care.

What is that thing that fills you with joy? Resolve to do it—even in a small way—this week. If you don't have time for a camping trip, take a walk in the closest green space. Maybe you can't afford a day at the spa, but why not take a relaxing bath? You need time for yourself. Take time to rest and rejuvenate so you can show up for yourself and your loved ones.

....

Remind me to take time for myself, Father. I ask that You would etch self-care on my heart and that You would continue to speak life into my long days. I'm grateful that You are never too weary to hear from me. May today be a time of rich communion with You.

When they measure themselves by one another and compare
themselves with one another, they are without understanding.
2 CORINTHIANS 10:12 ESV

We all do it. We compare homes, jobs, kids, physical appearances, and our ability to "do it all." We compare personalities, faith, possessions, talents, and income levels—and the only result is an envious, ungrateful heart. Comparison may begin innocently, but it can easily take over your thoughts—and, consequently, your actions.

Do you want to be freed from the trap of comparison? Instead of focusing on what you do not have, be grateful for all that you do have. Every morning, list a few things you are grateful for, whether it's your current workplace, your light-filled home, your ability to make others laugh, or the freckles that sprinkle your face in the summer. The more you open your eyes to all you have, the less likely you'll be to dwell on what you don't have. Freedom from comparison and competition is possible, and with it comes the fresh air of peace and contentment.

....

I struggle with comparison, Lord, and I then become ungrateful. I'm sorry.
Why do I fall into this trap and lose my heart of thankfulness? Please have
mercy on me. Help me to be content in You. Give me eyes to see all Your
blessings.

....

....

....

....

....

....

....

....

....

....

....

....

....

....

....

....

....

....

....

....

My soul is weary with sorrow; strengthen
me according to your word.

PSALM 119:28

When you're weary, everything is hard. Getting up in the morning is hard; being patient is hard; excelling at work is hard. Bone-deep weariness can leave you feeling wrung out and hopeless. Weary traveler, you can take a break.

God knows that your energy is spent and that you can't live the rest of your life in this kind of exhaustion. And He also knows exactly how you feel. If you're feeling deeply weary today, ask for help. You don't have to do it all, and the truth is, you can't do it all.

Pray to God for comfort. Call your closest friend and ask for help. Ask your spouse or family member for an ear; tell your church (or your boss, or your teammate) you need some time off. When you're weary, don't force yourself to keep going in hopes that you'll find rest eventually. Find rest now. Ask for help.

....

Lord, I am utterly exhausted. I want to put my trust in You, but I often fail. Show me the right path, and I will walk in it. Please send people and encouragement my way to help me find strength. Thank You for the family of God.

....

....

....

....

....

....

....

....

....

....

....

....

....

....

....

....

....

....

....

....

....

"Seek his kingdom, and these things will be given to you as well."

LUKE 12:31

When you're worried, the stress can easily take over your life. Your thoughts drift in conversation, your heart beats faster, and you feel anxious and overwhelmed.

What is it that you're anxious about today? Is it your job? Is it money? Measuring up to colleagues? Finding a spouse? Raising a family? Current events on the news?

Have no doubt, the Lord knows your worries and anxieties. He hears you when you're afraid and hurting, and He wants to take this burden you're carrying. Cry out to Him today. Be specific, and ask Him to free you from your anxiety. His response may not be instant—you might not even feel very different at first—but you can be sure that the Lord is moving heaven and earth to rescue you. All you need to do is call out to Him. Give Jesus your worry today. It's never too much for Him to handle, and He will give you peace.

....

Please help me release my worries to You, Lord. Remind me that You're in control. When my heart is anxious, help me trust in You. When I feel afraid, help me turn to You. Please give me the strength I need to render my fears inactive.

Will you not revive us again, that your people may rejoice in you?
PSALM 85:6

S top and smell the roses" is a saying you've probably heard before, but do you ever actually do it? All of creation beckons you to stop hurrying and instead to notice the beauty around you—the beauty that's so easy to miss as you scurry on by.

We are all guilty of this. How often do you drive to work not even noticing the sunrise? In the grocery store, do you ever pause to admire the rows of juicy purple grapes or the cheerful bouquets of flowers? It's easy to say, "Stop and smell the roses," but it's much harder to actually do it.

Today, and throughout your day, challenge yourself to slow down and notice the beauty around you. You may feel as if you don't have the time, but the simple act of slowing down, even for a moment, can bring a fresh perspective. Slow down and embrace God's gift of creation today. It will serve your spirit, and it will fuel your soul.

....

Remind me, Lord, even in my busiest moments, to slow down and notice the wonder around me. When I fail to recognize the simple moments, I miss out on You. I don't want to be so hurried that I don't see the beauty around me and relish in the God who made it.

....
....
....
....
....
....
....
....
....
....
....
....
....
....
....
....
....
....
....
....
....
....

Wise friends make you wise.
PROVERBS 13:20 CEV

*H*ow often does someone confess a struggle, a hardship, or a disappointment in their life and you respond with, "I had no idea"? If you're like most people, it happens a lot. In our culture, we so often put on a brave face—and we're so good at it—that no one knows the battle within.

Do your friends and family know you are craving more peace in your life? If not, tell them. Share some of your struggles with work-life balance, juggling a family and home, and your endless to-do list. Let someone in on the fact that you could use some prayer. Being vulnerable can help you, and your circle, work through emotions easier and become braver and more resilient.

Today, don't be afraid to ask others to help you in your quest to have fuller peace, deeply and intentionally. Delegate responsibilities in the workplace, and organize your days well. Peace can be yours, but sometimes you need a little help from your friends.

....

Lord, please fill my life with people who will help me find peace alongside my full life of busyness, work, and sometimes stress. Remind me that faith grows in fellowship and that I need to allow people in to the difficult parts of my journey.

Teach me knowledge and good judgment,
for I trust your commands.

PSALM 119:66

W hen you are in the presence of someone you don't trust, how do you act? Your guard is probably up, while your mind sifts through that person's intentions, actions, and words. You are on high alert.

But when you're with someone you trust, your demeanor is completely different. You're relaxed. Your words spill out comfortably, and you breathe deeply and laugh with ease. You feel at rest. Trust is a game changer.

When you trust the Lord with your plans, fears, hopes, and aspirations, you can relax. You can rest. He is more trustworthy than anyone in the universe, and you can rest assured that He wants only the very best for you. Trust isn't a blind free fall into the Lord's arms. It's a bold and confident leap that comes from knowing He's been faithful to His people for thousands of years. Trust Him and His good plans today. Whether you're at home, at work, or off on an adventure, let Him give you rest.

....

I trust and adore You, my Father and King. I rest in Your presence. Bring confidence to my heart as I put my faith in You. Where my heart is anxious, fill me with Your presence.

The LORD gives strength to his people; the
LORD blesses his people with peace.
PSALM 29:11

We like to stay connected. We like to know what new work trends are, what our competition is brewing, what our friends are up to, and what the latest news headlines are. And all this information is available at any time with the touch of a screen.

But staying connected, even with colleagues, can become an obsession. Do you panic if you don't have your phone? Are you constantly scrolling through your work emails or social media feeds? Are you reading news headlines more than your Bible? It's easy to get caught up in the trap of being "connected."

To find peace—the kind that recharges mind, body, and spirit—you may need to unplug. Turn off your phone. Close your email. Set aside your screens and look, instead, into the eyes of your family. Listen to the wind in the trees, and laugh at a silly joke. Unplugging from work is hard to do, but it is so beneficial. And once you do, you will find rest for your mind and soul.

....

Lord, help me seek peace and refreshment in Your presence, not in excess work or online noise. Remind me that Your voice is still and small and I can meet with You at any time. Help me remove barriers to hearing You clearly.

Keep your lives free from the love of money and be
content with what you have, because God has said,
"Never will I leave you; never will I forsake you."
HEBREWS 13:5

I f you battle against wanting to buy and buy some more, you're not alone. Consumerism is a real struggle for many, especially after a long workweek for mom. Advertisements, social media, and simply the act of living well all stir up the desire for more.

After finishing a big work project or a long week picking up kids, you might feel an urge to shop. When you see an ad for a flash sale or steep discount, you may go running for your credit card. But stop and think first, *What would it look like to pause from consumerism?*

It looks different for everyone, but here are a few ideas. Buy nothing except necessities for two weeks. Avoid social media and other places where ads are prominent. Ask your friends to hold you accountable. Buying isn't bad, but when wanting more consumes you, it also steals your contentment. Have hope—with Christ—you can overcome all things. And without the idol of consumerism, your life will be more peaceful.

....

I want to break this cycle. I want to steward my finances well, and I want to grow in Your wisdom. Please fill me with contentment instead. Help me to see my true worth in Your eyes.

May the God of hope fill you with all joy and peace
as you trust in him, so that you may overflow
with hope by the power of the Holy Spirit.
ROMANS 15:13

Joy is contagious, isn't it? It feels good to be around people and colleagues who exude a deep-rooted joy. And interestingly, a life full of joy is a life full of rest and trust in God. True joy isn't dependent on circumstances, or personality, or temperament. Joy can be found by anyone.

When you're joyful, you rise above the circumstances around you. You might be in the middle of a difficult relationship, or you may have lost a loved one. Your job may be crummy, or your finances are bleak, but joy isn't contingent on any of those things. Joy is found in the Lord.

Joy knows that nothing is too difficult for God. He is near and ready to help in your time of need. He will never leave or forsake you. Joy is more than huge toothy smiles or constant laughter. Joy is believing that the Lord's strength is greater than any trial. Choose joy today and find rest.

....

I want that joy, Father—Your joy. Help me rise above my struggles and find true strength. Guide me into the deeper places of Your heart so that I can relish knowing that You alone satisfy. Let me dig roots inside Your Word.

....

....

....

....

....

....

....

....

....

....

....

....

....

....

....

....

....

....

....

Better the little that the righteous have
than the wealth of many wicked.

PSALM 37:16

I s it hard for you to be content in your home? Whether it's an apart-ment with roommates, a house with three kids, or a condo by the ocean, home is the place we lay our heads at night. It is our sacred space for peace after a long workweek. And sometimes it's the place we cri-tique the most.

Your furniture may be fine, but your neighbor's new leather sofa makes your couch suddenly look shabby. You don't mind being squeezed into a two-bedroom duplex until your family member buys a six-bedroom home. Your outdated kitchen cooks meals perfectly well, but when you see your colleague's brand-new oven, your oven just doesn't seem to do the job as well.

Contentment is hard. Even at home in the garden of Eden, Adam and Eve wanted more. And since then, the world has been broken. No, your home will never be perfect, and that's okay. Find contentment in your home—flaws and all—and find a better night's sleep at the end of a busy workday.

....

Jesus, instead of seeing the flaws in my home, help me see it with a grateful heart. Remind me to be positive when I walk in the door. Help me steward my home with contentment, grace, and blessing.

....

....

....

....

....

....

....

....

....

....

....

....

....

....

....

....

....

....

....

My heart is not proud, LORD, my eyes are not haughty;
I do not concern myself with great matters or things too
wonderful for me. But I have calmed and quieted myself.

PSALM 131:1–2

When you're worried or stressed, your breathing becomes different. Your breaths are small and shallow instead of deep and even, and you engage your shoulders instead of your diaphragm. Your jaw clenches.

You probably don't feel you have time for a massage or the spa, but you want to feel better. You want your body and mind to feel at rest. That's where inhaling, exhaling, and releasing come in.

If your breathing is shallow, take several deep breaths in a row. Let your breath expand your lungs and move your diaphragm. As you exhale, do so slowly and in a controlled manner. If your jaw is tense, move it back and forth and do some stretches with it; you may feel a little silly, but you will also feel better. Throughout the day, do this breathing and jaw check. If you feel tension, then inhale, exhale, release . . . and rest in your breathing.

Father, remind me to inhale, exhale, and release whenever I feel anxious. I release my worries, stress, and struggles to You. Fill me afresh with Your peace. Whether at work or at home, remind me to always find my breath in You.

....
....
....
....
....
....
....
....
....
....
....
....
....
....
....
....
....
....
....

Day 23

There is now no condemnation for those who are in Christ
Jesus, because through Christ Jesus the law of the Spirit who
gives life has set you free from the law of sin and death.

ROMANS 8:1–2

We all want to be loved, to be admired, and to receive applause for our successes. We want to have friends and relationships and the nod of approval from many, including coworkers. We don't want to be rejected.

But because we are broken people, rejection will inevitably rear its head. Your boss might not recommend you for the promotion; a budding friendship could turn ugly; you may find yourself left out and uninvited. Rejection happens, and it hurts. You may wonder if you should even keep trying or if it might be best to simply sit back and let life happen. Fear of rejection is real.

Are you struggling with that fear today? If so, rest in these words from Jesus: "Whoever believes and has decided to trust in Him [as personal Savior and Lord] is not judged [for this one, there is no judgment, no rejection, no condemnation]" (John 3:18 AMP). The Lord won't reject you. He is a safe place to rest.

....

Father, rejection makes me want to run and hide. Whether I succeed at home
or at work, please remind me of my worth in You. Thank You for never
rejecting me. As I grow in my relationship with You, please continue to
show me Your faithfulness.

....

....

....

....

....

....

....

....

....

....

....

....

....

....

....

....

....

....

....

....

....

"Take my yoke upon you and learn from me, for I am gentle
and humble in heart, and you will find rest for your souls."
MATTHEW 11:29

A re you weary, discouraged, stressed, or afraid? Does the busyness of your workweek ahead make you angry instead of excited? Come to the Lord, dear one. He wants all of your mess—your exhaustion, pain, frustrations, responsibilities, and sins. He wants to hear you call His name and ask Him for help—and He will be quick to rescue you.

Don't let one more moment come between you and the One who gave His life for you. Call on His name, and ask Him to relieve you of your burdens. In Scripture, Jesus clearly stated He wants to give His people rest—not just for a minute or an hour; not just for your time at home but also your time at work. He wants to give us complete and unending rest.

Jesus didn't say, "Come to Me when you have everything figured out." He simply said, "Come to Me" (Matthew 11:28 NKJV). Call out His name, and let Him take your burdens away and replace them with His love, joy, peace, and rest.

....

I can't do this on my own anymore, Lord, and I'm asking You for help. Res-
cue me with Your peace. Help me to return to rest while at home, at work, or
among friends. Make my heart still in Your love, and allow me the perspec-
tive to know when to let go.

....
....
....
....
....
....
....
....
....
....
....
....
....
....
....
....
....
....
....
....
....

Even youths grow tired and weary, and young men stumble and fall; but those who hope in the LORD will renew their strength.

ISAIAH 40:30–31

How are you feeling physically? Does your body feel worn out? Is fatigue your constant companion? Do you collapse into bed at the end of the workday? You need rest, and you need it now.

Listen to your body. Rest is not a sign of weakness. In fact, recognizing and acting on the need for physical rest is one of the best things you can do for your body. If you're utterly exhausted, it's time to slow down.

Find solitude in a quiet place every day. It might be on your couch in the early morning hours before work, or it may come late at night, after everyone else is in bed. Instead of adding one more event to the calendar, add rest. It may mean saying no—even to some good things—but you'll be saying yes to peace. Be still in the quiet, let the day's worries roll off your shoulders, and allow your body and mind to settle. You will be able to show up as your best self if you take time to take care of yourself.

....

Father, help me remember to take advantage of these quiet times with You. Before I head out the door for a busy day of work, please give me the grace to sit in Your peace. Remind me to pause, to pray, and to breathe.

Restore our fortunes, LORD, like streams in the Negev.

PSALM 126:4

No one likes to fail. But at some point in our lives, we all do. Maybe you've already snapped at your children three times today or you completely forgot about that important meeting and didn't prep for it at all. Perhaps you shared someone's secret, did poorly on a work presentation, or forgot your loved one's birthday.

Sometimes we're so afraid of failing that we try to be in control of every detail. We believe complete control is the key to avoiding failure. But this is an illusion because we can never truly be completely in control.

The fact is, you will fail. You will mess up and make mistakes, even at work. Apologize, forgive yourself, and move on. Don't battle for control; instead, let the Lord guide your steps. Talk with Him throughout the day. And when you fail, watch His grace step in and wash your mistakes away. Don't let the fear of failing reign over your life.

....

I mess up every day, Father. Cover me with Your grace, and remind me that You are in control. I give both my successes and my failures to You. I never want to stop trying, but I also want to slow down so that I can listen to You well.

....

....

....

....

....

....

....

....

....

....

....

....

....

....

....

....

....

....

....

....

Very early the next morning before daylight, Jesus got up
and went to a place where he could be alone and pray.

MARK 1:35 CEV

If you were to commit a whole day off work to simply be, would you feel guilty? Many people would. But resting shouldn't go hand in hand with guilt.

Give yourself permission to pause, and enjoy it without piling on guilt. Self-care will make you healthier, happier, and more relaxed. In fact, a well-rested person is more productive and successful than a tired, stressed, and overwhelmed person.

If you feel guilty about taking time for yourself, remember that Jesus rested. He rested so that He could minister more effectively, and He invited His disciples into that peace with Him. Even though there were people who wanted to hear Him speak, He drew away from the crowds and made sure His human body was replenished. Peace is essential for your spiritual, emotional, and physical well-being; it also enhances your professional growth. It should not cause guilt.

Plan a time to take off during this workweek, and enjoy it. Giving yourself a break is a gift from God!

Lord, I feel guilty when I try to rest. Help me remember that peace is a gift from You. Enjoying Your peace is worth every minute, and I need to make it a priority. I can't pour from an empty cup, and sometimes I need that reminder. Please replenish me.

....

....

....

....

....

....

....

....

....

....

....

....

....

....

....

....

....

....

....

....

....

In vain you rise early and stay up late, toiling for
food to eat—for he grants sleep to those he loves.

PSALM 127:2

In 2018 Welch's commissioned a study to find out how many hours on average a working mom clocks.[1] The answer: approximately 98 hours. A working mom does the equivalent of about 2.5 full-time jobs in a week. The study also found that moms don't usually finish their work and family duties until after 8:00 p.m. We live in a culture where overworking is the norm—and it's a shame!

You are probably familiar with this tendency. Whether you're just starting out, are newly promoted, or are in a secure job, you may feel a constant pressure to prove yourself. But the question is, do you want to spend your life overworked and with no time to truly enjoy life?

Most would answer no. We want to know that, at the end of our lives, we loved deeply and lived fully. Dear friend, as much as you can, resist the urge to overwork. Yes, you may receive some pushback. But stand strong, and you'll walk out of the office every day knowing that you chose a full life—not an overworked life.

....

Lord, help me resist the urge to overwork. I want to focus on living a full life that honors You and brings peace to myself and my family. Give me the strength to create boundaries around my time so that I can be present with those I love most.

....

....

....

....

....

....

....

....

....

....

....

....

....

....

....

....

....

....

*For in six days the LORD made the heavens and the earth, the
sea, and all that is in them, but he rested on the seventh day.
Therefore the LORD blessed the Sabbath day and made it holy.*

EXODUS 20:11

When God included the command to rest in the Ten Commandments, He didn't add a disclaimer of "only if you have time for it." The Lord Himself made time for rest after the creation of the world. And for us, rest simply isn't an option.

The mindset of being constantly busy is considered normal in today's world, but endless busyness is not what the Lord commanded of us. Yes, He wants you to work hard, but He also wants you to rest. He wants you to take a break from the demands of life and recharge. When was the last time you did that?

This week be sure to follow the Lord's loving command. Even if there are things left undone, even when items are still on your to-do list, even if it looks as if rest is the last thing you should be doing, let it be first. Say a prayer and take a breath. Other things can wait until that is accomplished.

....

*Father God, often I ignore Your command to rest. But here I am, Lord;
please help me to be at peace in You and find You in prayer. Guide me into
Your love so that I can be obedient and enjoy the gift of Your presence.*

....
....
....
....
....
....
....
....
....
....
....
....
....
....
....
....
....
....
....
....
....

*"Do not work for food that spoils, but for food that endures
to eternal life, which the Son of Man will give you."*

JOHN 6:27

*S*ocrates once said, "He who is not contented with what he has,
would not be contented with what he would like to have." So
often we think that if we just had a new house, different job, new
wardrobe, better behaved kids, more money, or even a different spouse,
we would be happier—we would be content. But would we?

Contentment is a choice. It doesn't magically appear. It doesn't
automatically come with a new job or a new pair of jeans. If you want
contentment—and a break from feelings of discontent—you must
choose it.

Choosing to be content begins with gratitude. If you focus on what
you don't have, you immediately become less grateful for all you do
have. The Lord knows it's a struggle, and He also wants to untangle
you from the trap of discontentment. Call on Him today. Ask Him to
give you freedom, contentment, and peace in your life, in your family,
and in your work.

....

*Oh, Father, I struggle with being content. Please free me from the trap of
jealousy and discontentment. Remind me of the joy of Your presence, the
peace of Your heart, and the love of obedience.*

....

....

....

....

....

....

....

....

....

....

....

....

....

....

....

....

....

....

....

....

....

I will boast all the more gladly about my weaknesses,
so that Christ's power may rest on me.

2 CORINTHIANS 12:9

Perfection is unattainable. Ever since Adam and Eve sinned in the garden of Eden, life simply has not been perfect. Yet a lot of us seek perfection in our lives. We want a perfect life, perfect marriage, perfect job, and perfect house. We want to look fashionable, and we want to succeed in everything we do. We can strive for perfection as though it were attainable, but we will end up exhausted.

The good news is that God doesn't demand perfection from you. He knows you can't be faultless, and that's why He sent Jesus to die for you. Jesus was perfect for you—in your place. And the best thing you can do is to pray with Him every day, ask Him to lead you, and then follow His leading. You can do everything to the best of your ability, but you'll never be perfect. And that's okay. Rest from perfectionism today at home, at work, and in all things.

....

Father, please remind me that I can rest from performing because Jesus
lived a blameless life for me. Every day, I can call on You and accept Your
gift of salvation. Over and over again, You delight in rescuing me. Help me
remember You love me unconditionally.

....

....

....

....

....

....

....

....

....

....

....

....

....

....

....

....

....

....

....

✿✿✿✿✿ Day 32 ✿✿✿✿✿

"Who of you by worrying can add a single hour
to your life? Since you cannot do this very little
thing, why do you worry about the rest?"

Luke 12:25–26

W hat would you happen if you took a day off work? Would your family still function if you went away for one day? Would your ministry fail if you retreated to a quiet place for the weekend? One of our biggest fears about rest is this: If we take a break, we'll fall behind. Our competitors will get ahead; our families will fall to pieces; our ministries will be neglected.

When you take breaks, you are strengthened. Sabbaticals energize you and restore your soul. Balance can only do you good—and you'll return with a new zest for life.

Your world will not end if you take a day off to maintain peace. You may have to work a little harder before or after, and time off might feel strange, but God is in charge of the time. You will end up a better worker, mother, or minister if you take the time to recharge. And the Lord will bless your efforts to rest.

....

God, I confess that I'm afraid of falling behind if I take time off. Please give me courage to rest in You. Please help me know that rest in You is always more productive than my own plans of action.

$$\text{Day } 33$$

*How long, O Lord? Will you forget me forever? How long will
you hide your face from me? . . . But I have trusted in your
steadfast love; my heart shall rejoice in your salvation. I will
sing to the Lord, because he has dealt bountifully with me.*
PSALM 13:1, 5–6 ESV

The psalmist David made lots of mistakes and suffered the consequences. He often felt far from God, and at times, he even despaired.

Are you going through a painful time in your life? Is your heart broken into a million pieces, and do you wonder if it will ever be whole again? You may be suffering physical pain, or perhaps you've lost a loved one. Maybe you are experiencing depression, or you have missed out on a dream job or promotion. There are many ways pain can appear in our lives, and it can feel like an impossible burden. Take heart, dear one, for when life is painful, the Lord is right beside you.

God isn't far away, up in the sky, ignoring you. Rather, He is bearing the pain right along with you. He is wrapping His arms around you, experiencing your heartbreak with you, and shedding tears with you. Ask Him for His healing presence, His redemption, and His restoration.

*Help me, Lord, to find my strength in You. Give me grace, mercy, and truth
for this season. Comfort me in Your wisdom and strength. Heal me with
Your steadfast love.*

....

....

....

....

....

....

....

....

....

....

....

....

....

....

....

....

....

....

....

....

Unless the LORD builds the house, the builders labor in vain.
PSALM 127:I

*P*roductivity is a word used proudly. The more we get done in a day or week, the more accomplished we feel. Long workdays are often expected, and working on the weekends is the norm. In a society where productivity is king and time off is dismissed as unnecessary, how do we find respite from the constant going, going, going?

We simply have to do it. We rest. We rest without hesitation and without guilt. We take time off from work and obligations to enjoy our families, our God, and His creation. Peace is essential for working moms—our culture might not want to admit it, but it's true.

You may feel as if your world will come crashing down if you're not productive. You might feel as if it's impossible to rest if your to-do list isn't finished. You might even feel lazy or worthless if you take time for yourself. Push those thoughts out of your head because your joy is essential—God can handle everything else.

....

God, I am afraid to rest and feel unproductive. Show me that when I am at peace, the world benefits. Remind me that we can love only because You loved first. I can do nothing outside Your strength. Help me slow down and listen.

....

....

....

....

....

....

....

....

....

....

....

....

....

....

....

....

....

....

....

....

....

*"You will seek Me and find Me, when you
search for Me with all your heart."*

JEREMIAH 29:13 NKJV

Imagine your favorite dessert. Is it a warm, gooey brownie straight from the oven or a tangy lemon bar topped with powdered sugar? Maybe it's a slew of Oreos with milk or a cupcake topped with decadent frosting. Now imagine your dessert during rush-hour traffic. Your shirt is covered with crumbs; half the Oreos fall under the seat; you choke on the cupcake as traffic slams to a stop. Doesn't sound very enjoyable, does it?

But what if you picture yourself sitting in your comfiest chair, slowly savoring each bite? You have a hot coffee or tea next to you, and you get the opportunity to taste every layer of your treat. It's sweet and satisfying. That's a completely different experience, isn't it?

Your experience with God is similar. If you hurry through your time with Him, let distraction take over, or try to multitask in your prayer life, you won't enjoy the experience nearly as much. But if you take meaningful, intentional time to enjoy the Lord and His Word, you'll find relief from stress and worries—and you'll find deep peace within.

....

Help me not to rush my time with You, Lord, but to be more intentional about praying and listening to Your still, small voice. Remind me to slow down and savor Your presence.

....

....

....

....

....

....

....

....

....

....

....

....

....

....

....

....

....

....

....

....

~~~~~~~ *Day 36* ~~~~~~~

"Be still, and know that I am God."

PSALM 46:10

Twenty years ago, if you looked around a restaurant, you would see couples, families, and friends talking, laughing, and enjoying being together. Today, however, you'll see many diners on their phones—texting, scrolling social media, and checking their email.

Technology has helped us in many ways, and we should be grateful for its role in our lives. But technology shouldn't be our lives.

Think about your time at the dinner table after a long day of work. Are you engaging with your family or friends? When you're eating solo, are you intentionally enjoying the moment? Or does your dinnertime involve your phone or another device? Are you looking at your screen more than the faces of your family? Instead of enjoying your meal and reveling in the flavors, are you mindlessly scrolling through your social media feeds?

Limiting your interaction with technology at dinnertime will help you connect more with God, yourself, and others—and your eyes and brain will be grateful for the break.

....

God, help me use dinnertime for connection with You and those around me. Remind me to enjoy presence over media, peace over busyness, and people over technology.

....

....

....

....

....

....

....

....

....

....

....

....

....

....

....

....

....

....

....

He leads me beside quiet waters, he refreshes my soul.
PSALM 23:2–3

If you lead a busy life, you may be craving time for yourself, but you never seem to have any. Your schedule fills up with work, social outings, family, errands, and more. Then, before you know it, you're going to bed an hour later than you were hoping.

Often, the only way to find time for yourself is to guard it. This time should be a nonnegotiable, treasured, and protected part of your day or week. Nothing except an emergency should take its place—even if your friends are having a last-minute movie night or your child wants an impromptu playdate or you've just realized you're out of milk. Zealously guard that hour or two just for yourself—those other things can wait—and you'll feel more rested, energized, and calm as a result.

Your time as a working mom is valuable, so guard it well. You won't regret it.

....

Remind me to guard my time, Lord, especially in moments of busyness and stress. Bless my day, my schedule, and my time for rest. I want to honor You with my presence.

....

....

....

....

....

....

....

....

....

....

....

....

....

....

....

....

....

....

....

....

Consider him who endured such opposition from sinners,
so that you will not grow weary and lose heart.

HEBREWS 12:3

When you take time off or say no, you aren't letting other people down. You may have said no to the extra work project, birthday party invitation, church service opportunity, or another event. Saying no to those requests means you said yes to something very important—you! You said yes to your peace, your well-being, and your mental health.

Are you afraid that if you take time to take care of yourself, you'll be viewed as lazy? Do you think that everything will fall apart if you aren't there to control it? Be assured peace will only do you good. Caring for yourself is just as important as fulfilling work obligations or tending to the needs of others—and you won't be effective at serving others if your body and mind are tired. You must fill up your cup if you want to fill the cups of others.

Today, remind yourself that rest is a good choice. You are not letting anyone down, and you are certainly not letting God down. Ask God to help you see this truth and to rest in it.

....

Father, I am afraid to rest because I fear others' disapproval. Please show me how to rest without fear. I want to find my peace in You and know that it's good for me to care for myself.

....

....

....

....

....

....

....

....

....

....

....

....

....

....

....

....

....

....

....

....

I urge you, brothers and sisters, in view of God's mercy, to
offer your bodies as a living sacrifice, holy and pleasing
to God—this is your true and proper worship.

ROMANS 12:1

How can jogging three miles or biking for an hour be calming? Physical exercise may tire out your body, but it does wonderful things—calming things—for your mind. If you are overwhelmed with the demands in your life, you may want to consider putting on your tennis shoes.

Getting your heart rate up, working up a sweat, and pushing yourself physically can actually help you unwind after a long day at the office. If you're stressed and try to combat it by moping around the house and eating potato chips, you may actually become even more anxious because your mind is focusing on stress. However, when you exercise, you'll produce more endorphins, get better sleep, and receive an energy boost .

If you feel worn down and discouraged, you may just need to work up a sweat—and through it, you'll find peace and joy.

....

Creator God, inspire me to take care of my body and find balance for my
overwhelmed mind. Remind me that honoring You with my movement is a
way to express worship and praise.

....

....

....

....

....

....

....

....

....

....

....

....

....

....

....

....

....

....

....

....

Return to your rest, my soul, for the LORD has been good to you.

PSALM 116:7

There are so many products, procedures, books, and seminars that promise to make you better—more beautiful, more youthful, more confident, more productive, more financially stable. With all of those promises bombarding us, we can easily become discontented with who we are.

Some days more than others, you need to remember that you're a child of God. He created you with quirks, talents, and a one-of-a-kind personality. You are uniquely you. While it's good to work toward achieving goals and being your best, it's also important to remember that you are enough.

When you look in the mirror today, or compare yourself to someone else at work, or wish you were somehow different, take a moment to tell yourself, "I am enough." God loves you simply because you are you. You don't have to become someone else in order for God to love you. Remember that you are enough, and rest in that truth today.

....

Lord, help me find peace in knowing that You love me simply because I am Your child. Whether at home, at work, or in my community, please give me ears to hear that You have created me uniquely. I want to care for myself in the way You have designed me.

....

....

....

....

....

....

....

....

....

....

....

....

....

....

....

....

....

....

....

....

....

Make your face shine upon your servant,
and teach me your statutes.
PSALM 119:135 ESV

When you look at your calendar, do you ever get a sinking feeling in your stomach? Each morning is filled with work, and every evening has some type of commitment. Sometimes there's not much you can do about having a busy, filled-to-the-brim week. But you can control how you respond. And you can still find peace—it just may look a little different.

Look for pockets of peace. Stuck in the car? Turn on some worship music or simply sit in silence, soaking in the Lord's presence. Do you have back-to-back meetings all day? Take just a few moments in between to practice deep breathing—you'll enter your meetings calmer and refreshed. If you're serving in your church's Sunday service, take a minute beforehand to praise God for His sacrifice.

You may feel weary when you look at the week ahead, but know there is peace waiting for you—even when your calendar is full.

....

When I am overwhelmed during this busy week, Father, help me find moments of peace in Your presence. Whether in work or family life, help me to remember You in all that I do.

....

....

....

....

....

....

....

....

....

....

....

....

....

....

....

....

....

....

....

....

....

....

[Do] not giv[e] up meeting together, as some are in
the habit of doing, but encourag[e] one another—and
all the more as you see the Day approaching.

HEBREWS 10:25

It's not easy to ask for help. Our society prides itself on self-sufficiency. We look with envy at those who seem to "do it all." Asking for help may make us feel weak or embarrassed, especially at work, and we don't want to burden others with our needs or inadequacies.

Asking for help requires vulnerability. But by taking a risk and being vulnerable, you encourage others to be vulnerable too. And wouldn't you like to have people around you who are open about their struggles rather than just putting on a brave face every day? It might be up to you to begin the movement.

Ask someone in your circle for help. It might be a best friend, a coworker, or a spouse. It may be someone from church or from your small group, a family member or even your boss. You don't need to feel ashamed. In fact, you'll probably discover that you aren't alone in your struggles. So ask for help, and when help arrives, accept it.

....

It's hard to ask for help, Lord. Please give me the courage to be vulnerable. Remind me that every person needs help once in a while. It's good to reach out to others.

....

....

....

....

....

....

....

....

....

....

....

....

....

....

....

....

....

....

....

....

....

....

....

Some trust in chariots and some in horses, but
we trust in the name of the LORD our God.

PSALM 20:7

You swipe your credit card to pay for groceries and inwardly wince. You put your tithe in the offering plate at church and pray the Lord will provide. You try to pick up as much extra work as possible, and you're an expert at coupons. Still, your finances look bleak.

If you're wrestling with money worries, hear these words: *God knows your needs.* He knows how much those car repairs will cost, how long you'll be searching for a new job, and when the next tuition payment is due. He's intimately involved in your life, and He cares deeply about you and your well-being.

Take a deep breath and feel the air rush through your lungs. The Lord—who formed your airways and the very oxygen molecules that fill them—knows everything you need, and He promises to provide. Cling to His promises today. When your finances look grim, rest in the provision of the cross.

....

You promise to provide for me, Lord, and I am choosing to trust Your words. Help me to trust You with my finances, and help me to believe in Your salvation in every aspect of my life.

Two are better than one, because they have a good return for
their labor: If either of them falls down, one can help the other
up. But pity anyone who falls and has no one to help them up.
ECCLESIASTES 4:9–10

The best of friends make you feel at home. You feel safe seeing them no matter how crazy your day is and no matter what you're wearing. All pretenses dissolve, and you can tell them anything.

Other relationships might be more difficult, including work relationships. You may feel like you constantly need to prove yourself, that you always need to put your best foot forward, and that you need to cover up your insecurities. Does this describe any of your relationships? Do you feel like some of them require constant work to maintain? If so, ask the Lord to bring restful friendships into your life.

As Proverbs 17:17 says, "A friend loves at all times." A friend loves you when you're a hot mess and when you confess your mistakes. A friend loves through good times and hard times. A true friend doesn't disappear. A friend should bring peace, not stress, to your life. Thank God for your peaceful friendships, especially outside your work life.

....

Lord, will You bring to my life specific people who are willing to live a life of
peace with me? Help me to have friends outside of work who can encourage
me in my home life and in my career.

On my bed I remember you; I think of you through
the watches of the night. Because you are my
help, I sing in the shadow of your wings.

PSALM 63:6–7

Going to bed might seem like an obvious way to rest, but it's easier said than done. If you work full days, evenings may be the only time to connect with your spouse or kids. Evenings might be your only alone time throughout the day, and if you're an introvert, alone time is especially crucial. You might have time to see friends only after work, and if you're an extrovert, you especially need that social stimulation. And sometimes, the book you're reading is just too good to put down.

Those are all valid reasons not to go to bed—and they are also why going to bed requires discipline. Observing a set bedtime requires a firm commitment to getting an adequate amount of sleep so your body isn't physically tired.

Sometimes rest involves sacrifice. Decide on a reasonable hour for bedtime and stick to it. You'll be amazed how rested you'll feel in the morning when you go to work.

....

God, I know I need more sleep. Please give me the discipline to go to bed on time so I can have full and healthy days. Bring my body into its best personal rhythm for my relationship with You so that I can live and breathe and have my being in You.

....

....

....

....

....

....

....

....

....

....

....

....

....

....

....

....

....

....

....

....

....

....

Am I now trying to win the approval of human beings, or of
God? Or am I trying to please people? If I were still trying
to please people, I would not be a servant of Christ.
GALATIANS 1:10

We all love approval. We all love to be loved. It's intoxicating and addictive, and it boosts our self-esteem by leaps and bounds. But too many of us seek others' approval more than we seek God's approval.

When we set out to gain the approval of others, it can turn into a never-ending quest. That's because the minute we earn someone's approval—whether that person is our boss, friend, spouse, parent, significant other, or teacher—we're off and searching for someone else's too. We want that stamp of approval from everyone, and that can be exhausting.

It's natural to want to be liked. We want others to think highly of us, and we want to be respected, especially at work. But first and foremost, we need to seek God's approval. His opinion is ultimately the only one that matters. His approval allows us to rest securely and safely in His eternal love and His everlasting grace.

....

Instead of seeking the approval of other people, Lord, may I strive to know
and please You. Whether at work or at home, remind me that Your opinion
is the one that matters.

....

....

....

....

....

....

....

....

....

....

....

....

....

....

....

....

....

....

Day 47

The fear of the LORD leads to life; then one
rests content, untouched by trouble.

PROVERBS 19:23

We often associate the word *gratitude* with Thanksgiving. While the turkey is passed, we talk about what we're thankful for, and then we often forget for the rest of the year. But why not focus on gratitude every day, especially as a working mom?

Though it may seem trite or childish, counting our blessings is clearly linked with rest. When we count our blessings, we realize how much we do have. And by listing the things we're thankful for, we are less apt to focus on what we don't have.

A grateful heart is a heart at rest. It doesn't want more. It doesn't feel the need to show off or compete or work harder. It is content. Can you say that about yourself?

Today, notice the blessings around you, especially at work. Open your eyes to this wondrous world you live in. You'll find your heart less inclined to covet and envy, and instead, you'll find a peace that passes all understanding. It is the place of contentment and peace.

....

Lord, teach me to see the many blessings You bring me every day. While at work, help me give thanks for the purpose and relationships I have in my job. Remind me that a life of healthy productivity is a gift in itself.

....

....

....

....

....

....

....

....

....

....

....

....

....

....

....

....

....

....

....

....

*How good and pleasant it is when God's
people live together in unity!*
PSALM 133:1

Who do you go to when you have a prayer request? Or when you're having a hard day at work? Or when you simply need help? If certain individuals pop into your head, those people are your community. They're the ones who can help you find peace in tangible ways—and they're the ones with whom you can risk being vulnerable.

Being vulnerable isn't a comfortable feeling in today's do-it-yourself society. But once you risk being honest and vulnerable with someone, chances are that person will risk being honest and vulnerable with you too.

Perhaps you've just had surgery and need help with meals; ask your friend for a meal train. Maybe you're struggling with extra responsibilities at work and need an extra hand with your kids; ask your neighbor for a favor. Or perhaps you're weary of searching for a needed new job; ask your community for prayers. Be brave enough to risk asking for help—to risk being vulnerable. And when you feel rested, be sure to return the favor.

....

Lord, it's hard to ask for help. Give me the courage to be vulnerable with my community. As a working mom, help me lean on You and also trusted friends who can help me carry the loads of life.

ᘓᘓᘓᘓᘓᘓ **Day 49** *ᘒᘒᘒᘒᘒᘒ*

Stay focused; listen to the wisdom I have gained;
give attention to what I have learned about life.

PROVERBS 5:1 VOICE

Your alarm beeps and you wake up, automatically reaching to check your work email on your phone. You hear a buzzing noise and rummage in your bag for your phone. You need to check the time, so you grab your phone. And the list goes on.

There are so many ways your phone is helpful: it offers the time, directions, information, quick communication, and even video calls. There are countless apps to help with everything from tracking your daily steps to delivering your favorite pizza. Yet sometimes you just need to disconnect the phone and connect with God.

Disconnecting wasn't a needed concept when a phone was nothing more than a phone. But with the invention of smartphones and working at all hours, disconnecting is now a necessity.

Challenge yourself to disconnect today. Sit in silence and prayer. Pay attention to what the Lord is saying to you, and revel in the gift of quiet, preserved time.

....

Remind me, Lord, to disconnect from my phone and to connect with You. I repent for living a life of distraction, faulty connection, and media. Help me to be present, to live fully, and to pray without ceasing.

"I have told you these things, so that in me you may
have peace. In this world you will have trouble.
But take heart! I have overcome the world."

JOHN 16:33

*Y*ou might feel frazzled right now. Your brain is spinning a million miles an hour, and your email is full of work questions that you'll be up all night answering. You have so much to do that it feels like a stretch to even sit down and read these words. Sound familiar?

Stop. Just for a few minutes, let the world pass by. Time is ticking— and it is so very valuable—but even more precious is the time you spend with the Lord. Breathe deeply and calm your heart. Relax your breath, and let your mind become still.

Right now, in this moment, God wants you to give it all to Him— your busy schedule, your financial worries, the stress you're feeling at work, and the heartbreak you're nursing. He wants you to trust Him, and He wants you to trust that even as the world continues on, you're doing the right thing by resting in Him.

....

Father, help me step away from this world's busyness and rest in You. Work can wait. You are always there to meet with me, and sometimes I need a reminder to walk in Your presence instead of in my anxieties.

I lift up my eyes to the mountains—where does
my help come from? My help comes from the
LORD, the Maker of heaven and earth.

PSALM 121:1–2

Y ou're exhausted. There's no other way to put it. When you wake up, you want to go back to sleep. And when you fall asleep, your mind is still riddled with your work to-do list. You survive on coffee and adrenaline, meetings and video calls, and you crave peace like a desert wanderer craves water.

Friend, exhaustion is real. And this world can be overwhelming. Responsibility is all-consuming, and it may seem as if you'll never get a break as a working mom. Listen carefully: God does not want you to do it all. He doesn't want you to be so tired that you're barely hanging on to sanity.

Ask God for help today. Ask Him to lead you to someone—a sister, brother, parent, friend, neighbor, colleague, or fellow church member—who can ease your burden. Healing your body, mind, and soul of exhaustion is so much more important than looking as if you have it all together. You don't need to be exhausted any longer; help is on the way.

....

Jesus, I lift my eyes to You. I am exhausted and overwhelmed. Rescue me with Your care. Refresh me with Your healing, and guide me with Your grace. I need Your help, and I receive Your truth.

....
....
....
....
....
....
....
....
....
....
....
....
....
....
....
....
....
....

I have put my trust in you. Show me the way I should go.
PSALM 143:8

When you're putting together a puzzle, whether it's a hundred-piece puzzle or a thousand-piece puzzle, one thing remains true—you can't force the pieces together. Even when you think a piece belongs somewhere, if it doesn't fit, it simply won't work. You'll have to move on and find a piece that does fit.

And can't the same be said for our life plans? It can be tempting to force our own plans into action. When we know what we want (perhaps a promotion or a career move), and we think we have the right piece of the puzzle for it to work, we might try to force it into place. Then it can be easy not to understand why the job doesn't pan out or the dream isn't fulfilled.

If you're trying to force a puzzle piece to fit and it's not working, ask the Lord to show you the right piece. Rely on His expertise, and wait. After all, He's the master Puzzle-Maker, and He knows how to take seemingly disconnected pieces and turn them into a beautiful life.

....

Dear Lord, show me how to put the puzzle of this life together in a way that glorifies You. Help me to discern when to wait, when to move, and when to pray. I want Your will in all things I do.

"The LORD does not look at the things people look at. People look at the outward appearance, but the LORD looks at the heart."

I SAMUEL 16:7

Life is busy and full of achievements—and with it a flurry of photos on social media. Whether you use Twitter, Instagram, Facebook, or another platform, filtered photos are everywhere. You scroll through images of exotic cruises, job promotions, kitchen renovations, and relaxing beach resorts. And even though the pictures are beautiful, your heart may not be.

Envy creeps in. You want to either criticize your friends' photos—or criticize yourself for not having the picture-perfect life. Stop—and that's a command said in love.

That picture-perfect life isn't attainable. It's an illusion that keeps us striving and searching. There is only One who will truly satisfy, only One who perfectly measures up to God's standards: Jesus.

Rest in the truth that God doesn't look at your appearance, vacation photos, job promotions, or material wealth. He looks at your heart, and He invites you to reflect. So drop out of the social media competition and find quiet in your own circumstances.

....

Life is harder when I compare myself to others. Turn my eyes to You instead. Keep me free from the pitfalls of social media and lies that the grass is greener on the other side. You are faithful; help me to also be faithful.

....

....

....

....

....

....

....

....

....

....

....

....

....

....

....

....

....

....

....

....

If we have food and clothing, we will be content with that.

I TIMOTHY 6:8

Look around any bookstore, and you'll see bestsellers with titles boasting the words *stronger, calmer, richer, thinner, faster,* or *greater.* Our culture tells us we need to be better and have more—according to its standards. We need more success. We need more money. A better life lies in being thinner.

And every year we make resolutions that revolve around "more" and "better." *This will be the year,* we think. We mark the calendar, make a plan, buy a book, find accountability, and then, so often, we fail.

Yes, it's great to be healthier, more organized, more strategic, or more successful. But there's also danger in continually trying to meet the world's standards of more and better. It's all right to sometimes say, "I'm going to rest instead, and I'm going to look for 'more' and 'better' in the Lord." That isn't being lazy. It's being intentional with the time God has given you. Rest from more and better.

....

Lord, I get so caught up in the race of this world; help me rest from all my striving. I repent from trying to live a life that is based on performance instead of on the truth and mercy of Jesus.

....

....

....

....

....

....

....

....

....

....

....

....

....

....

....

....

....

....

....

....

....

....

....

"Your Father, who sees what is done in secret, will reward you."

MATTHEW 6:6

*R*ecognition is an enticing word. It feels good to be recognized for our efforts, whether it's as a spouse, parent, friend, colleague, or teacher. We like knowing that we're seen and valued. It can give us a boost of confidence in our abilities, life trajectories, and work. But seeking recognition sometimes leads to sin.

Constantly chasing recognition can leave you tired and frustrated. You worked so hard but still didn't get that promotion, or an undeserving colleague was named Employee of the Year. You went all out to make a healthy meal, and your kids just complained. You sent that family in need a check, and they never said thank you. You want to be acknowledged. You want to be applauded. You want to be . . . recognized.

It can be difficult to do things and feel like it doesn't matter. But God sees you, He knows you, and He blesses those who bless others. Keep doing what is good while also knowing God will show you when to respond and when to create boundaries.

....

God, You are the One I should be adoring. Forgive me for seeking recognition instead of seeking You. Help me to have proper boundaries while also giving generously. Be my motivation for life.

Do everything without grumbling or arguing, so that
you may become blameless and pure, "children of God
without fault in a warped and crooked generation." Then
you will shine among them like stars in the sky.

PHILIPPIANS 2:14–15

The grocery lines are too long, traffic is crazy, and your colleague made a remark that set your blood boiling. Your cereal was soggy, your car is too old, and your mother-in-law is driving you nuts. We voice so many complaints every single day. But is it worth it?

Often, complaining puts us in an even lower mood. And when complaining doesn't fix the issue, we complain again. A bad attitude can affect our self-worth, families, friends, and coworkers, as well as anyone who simply crosses our paths. Try something: stop speaking negatively.

Every time you start complaining, remind yourself to speak peacefully instead. Focus on the positive things in your life, job, and family. Take a deep breath and move on. Send up a prayer for God's protection over your words.

Complaining can be a full-time job, so today take a vacation—a permanent one—from complaining.

....

Lord, gently remind me to focus on the positive when I am tempted to
grumble. Help me release my fear and grief to You so that I can change my
words and my life.

....

....

....

....

....

....

....

....

....

....

....

....

....

....

....

....

....

....

We are God's handiwork, created in Christ Jesus to do good
works, which God prepared in advance for us to do.
EPHESIANS 2:10

You are a person, mother, sister, spouse, friend. You are gentle and loyal, feisty and funny, intelligent and strong. You are so many things wrapped into one body.

You are a delight. But you may not feel delightful. You may feel weak, discouraged, overwhelmed, or angry. You might even wish you were a completely different person. Maybe you want to be taller, thinner, richer, or calmer. But guess what? You're you, and there's no one else like you. You're individually made with unique gifts. Your mind, voice, laugh, and personality are wonderfully irreplaceable, whether at home or at work.

Stop trying to be someone you're not—and start being the person God created you to be: yourself. Sit with that thought today, and every time you begin to criticize yourself, ask your Maker for perspective. Embrace yourself, and find peace in who you are: a beloved child of God.

....

When I am tempted to be someone I'm not, remind me that I'm Your beloved child. Help me to live, love, and work from this perspective.

....

....

....

....

....

....

....

....

....

....

....

....

....

....

....

....

....

....

....

When anxiety was great within me, your
consolation brought me joy.

PSALM 94:19

A nxiety is real. It is all-consuming and paralyzing, and it often can make you feel out of control, isolated, and fearful. Maybe you experience it on a daily basis, or perhaps you have anxiety only when you're flying in an airplane or trying something new. Every person has varying degrees of anxiety in life, but the truth is simple: it can overtake you without the help of Jesus.

If you are feeling anxious today, there is hope. You can find rest from it. And you can overcome it. There will be a day when your heart won't race uncontrollably with life worries, work pressure, or family crises. There will be a time when you won't feel overwhelmed.

The first step to overcoming anxiety is to take action. Ask God for help, and then seek out a family member, friend, or counselor. Fill your mind with scriptures about God's peace. And find hope knowing that your panic will not last forever. You will find peace in Jesus.

....

Father, when anxiety from life or work threatens to consume me, lead me to
Your refuge and calm my troubled heart. Remind me of Your peace and give
me strength to receive You.

Sovereign LORD, *you are God! Your covenant is trustworthy,*
and you have promised these good things to your servant.

2 SAMUEL 7:28

You don't want your elderly parent to fall in their old age. Your friend is continually making bad financial decisions. Your co-worker lost her job. Your son is being bullied. Your daughter just received a scary diagnosis. Watching loved ones suffer, grow old, make bad choices, or struggle is scary and very difficult. It would be so much easier if you could be in control . . . or would it?

Are you worried about a loved one today? Is it making you anxious or causing you pain? Rest in the Lord's peace. He who holds the universe in His hands knows every detail of the situation. He knows the outcome, and He asks you to trust in His timing, provision, and comfort. You don't have to fix the world.

It's difficult, but it's also so very freeing to acknowledge that you don't have control. But you do have a God who loves you deeply and fully. He can give you peace, even from your deepest fears and heartaches. Pray, ask Him for provision for your loved ones, and let go.

Jesus, I commit everyone I love to Your able, steady, and loving hands. I know that You love them more than I do. I ask that You would enable me to be at peace with Your care and provision.

....
....
....
....
....
....
....
....
....
....
....
....
....
....
....
....
....
....

Then, because so many people were coming and going that
they did not even have a chance to eat, he said to them, "Come
with me by yourselves to a quiet place and get some rest."

MARK 6:31

I f you told a friend or colleague about your relaxing, restful, abso-
lutely renewing weekend, would you feel the need to apologize?
We're often quick to boast about our busyness, but we're hesitant to
talk about our need for balance. And then, when we do rest, we can feel
as if we've stolen the time or are undeserving.

Dear friend, be relieved of feeling guilty for taking time for yourself. You shouldn't harbor regrets for tending to your mind, body, and
soul. Remember, the Lord didn't apologize for resting after creation,
and He commands you to be still after work.

If you're ashamed of taking a break, be freed from that feeling.
Instead, bask in the energy, joy, and freedom that you receive from resting intentionally and well.

....

Lord, turn my heart toward seeking Your joy instead of worrying what
others may think. Help me to allow myself to take breaks from work, know-
ing that You will always be in the stillness that follows.

Let your face shine on your servant; save
me in your unfailing love.

PSALM 31:16

Because peace is important for our spiritual growth, Satan will do everything he can to keep us busy and distracted. One of the most common ways he ensures we don't rest is through guilt. Do you ever feel guilty if you take time to rest? As a working mother, you might always have a side of guilt hanging around, no matter how hard you try.

God worked for six days. He formed tall, sturdy oaks; poured light into fireflies; and made humans in His own image—and then, He rested. Without guilt and without shame. The Lord worked, and then He rested. The Lord did it as an example for His children. He takes care of us so we can Sabbath with Him.

When we rest, we aren't neglecting our duties, and we aren't being lazy. But we are giving our souls a chance to breathe and redirecting our minds to thoughts of the Lord. Sabbath benefits our physical bodies and our spiritual beings. It should be met with thanksgiving, not shame. Give thanks that the Lord knew we needed rest and so He created it at the beginning of time.

....

Take away my shame and guilt, dear Jesus, and help me enjoy the blessing
of peace. Remind me to take a Sabbath day, to rest in You, to be with You.
You are the Giver of life and peace.

....

....

....

....

....

....

....

....

....

....

....

....

....

....

....

....

....

....

....

....

....

Envy rots the bones.

PROVERBS 14:30

*E*nvy begins subtly, but then it "rots the bones." And like a weed, once it takes root, it spreads quickly and is hard to kill.

Our materialistic culture pushes the notion of never having enough, and many of us have come to believe this lie. When we see someone else looking happy, we want what they have. A beach vacation, perfect skin, a more impressive job title, a clean house, better-behaved children, a flawless body—the list goes on and on.

Envy is controlling, but it doesn't need to control you. It can be overcome. Find rest from envy, and you'll find contentment and richness in your own life and your own story. Instead of letting envy rot your bones, halt it before it can enter any part of your heart. Ask God to take every thought captive and fill you with gratitude instead—then relish gratitude for all the Giver has given you.

....

Please, Lord, take all my thoughts captive—especially the envious ones—and give me rest. Remind me of Your faithful love, and give me a heart of joy. Show me how to live my life so that I don't envy others around me.

....

....

....

....

....

....

....

....

....

....

....

....

....

....

....

....

....

....

....

....

Mak[e] the best use of the time, because the days are evil. Therefore do not be foolish, but understand what the will of the Lord is.

Ephesians 5:16–17 esv

ere's an important question to contemplate: "Is this the best use of my time?"

You may be surprised by how often your answer is no. After eliminating those ten minutes of social media scrolling, or half hour of stewing over a fight with your spouse, or an hour of mindlessly watching a television show you're only half interested in, you may find that you have more time in your day than you thought.

By asking yourself how you're using your time, you can fill the spaces you have freed up with something life-giving—like taking a nap, spending time in prayer, playing with your child, reconnecting with a loved one, or reading a good book. Or you could get some of life's necessities out of the way, like packing school lunches, prepping for a conference call, or balancing the budget—leaving you with more room for intentional peace.

....

Lord, remind me that time is fleeting, and guide me to a more intentional, rested life. Life is not all about work and busyness. Life is about connecting with You and living in obedience to You.

....
....
....
....
....
....
....
....
....
....
....
....
....
....
....
....
....
....

He will yet fill your mouth with laughter
and your lips with shouts of joy.

JOB 8:21

We all have difficult relationships at some point in our lives. Whether it's with our parents, siblings, neighbors, coworkers, friends, or children, relational turmoil is unavoidable. We are broken people, and we sometimes say and do hurtful things to one another.

Is there a tumultuous relationship in your life? A family member or colleague who pushes all the wrong buttons? Is it giving you anxiety or keeping you up at night? Do you have a knot in your stomach when you think about that person? If so, tell the Lord about it. Ask Him to reveal truth to your heart and the other person's heart as well.

Navigating broken relationships can be stressful, awkward, and painful. But when you are walking with the Lord, He can lift that burden from you and guide you along His perfect pathway. Ask Him to give you rest from this tough relationship today. And find freedom in knowing that He delights in walking alongside His children, even in the most difficult times.

....

Father, You love reconciliation. Family, friendships, and work relation-
ships are all important to You. Please bring peace to this difficult situation,
and show me how to love well.

....

....

....

....

....

....

....

....

....

....

....

....

....

....

....

....

....

....

....

....

....

*The LORD is my strength and my shield; my heart
trusts in him, and he helps me. My heart leaps
for joy, and with my song I praise him.*

PSALM 28:7

We live fast-paced lives. We want one-day shipping, five-minute prepped meals, emails instead of meetings, and instant results. Our society expects instant gratification, so when we have to wait, it can feel excruciating.

Are you waiting for an answer today? Maybe you've been longing for a job change or a promotion, but the answer so far seems to be no. Perhaps you're searching for a new house, trying to save for retirement, or waiting for a loved one to return from deployment. We wait in countless ways, and most of the time, our prayers are not instantly answered. And that's okay.

It's okay because God has a plan bigger than your own. He hears your prayers, and He knows your desires. He isn't ignoring you. He's simply working in His way and in His time. Stand confidently with the knowledge that God is good and loving and He loves to give you good gifts—they just aren't often overnighted.

....

*Help me trust that You want only good things for me, Lord—especially
while I am waiting. Give me a patient heart that can be still and trusting of
You. Show me the way of joy and self-control.*

Your beauty should not come from outward adornment,
such as elaborate hairstyles and the wearing of gold
jewelry or fine clothes. Rather, it should be that of your
inner self, the unfading beauty of a gentle and quiet
spirit, which is of great worth in God's sight.

I PETER 3:3–4

Are you striving to appear a certain way? Do you want others to think you're supermom, a powerful CEO, a woman who can do it all, or the church member with the perfect family? Those certainly aren't bad things, but is your striving taking over your life? Are you too busy worrying about how you look to find time to actually rest and be content with who you are?

The truth is, we all fall short. We all make mistakes and let others down. No one has it all together. And though we try to appear perfect, in fact, we are far from it.

The Bible says people look at the outward appearance, "but the LORD looks at the heart" (1 Samuel 16:7). Instead of chasing a perfect appearance, ask God to transform your heart and shift your mind away from pursuing an outer image that will never truly satisfy.

....

Heavenly Father, transform my heart from the inside out. Renew a right
spirit within me and cleanse my soul from sin. Feed me with truth, mercy,
and grace.

*"Blessed are those who trust in the Lord and have
made the Lord their hope and confidence."*

JEREMIAH 17:7 NLT

When your alarm clock begins blaring, the baby wakes up, or
your meeting is moved up, it's all too easy to begin your day in a
rush. But consider this—beginning with a calm mindset can transform
your entire day.

It is often in the quiet and stillness that we hear God's voice. When
we look to Him first thing in the morning, we acknowledge that we
cannot get through this day on our own strength. When we surrender
the day and all its frustrations, joys, and stresses to Him, we can rest,
knowing He is in control.

Begin your day looking up at the Lord instead of looking at your
own two feeble hands. Even if you only have a brief moment on one of
"those" mornings, breathe in His peace, His presence, and His provision. Be relieved of the burden of control. Have comfort in knowing
that the Lord walks with you.

....

*Bless me this morning, God, and remind me of Your presence throughout my
day today. Let me surrender my life to You in the small moments and in the
big ones, knowing that You are faithful. I can trust in You.*

....

....

....

....

....

....

....

....

....

....

....

....

....

....

....

....

....

....

....

*The LORD replied, "My Presence will go
with you, and I will give you rest."*
EXODUS 33:14

I t's a place we've all been in. You wanted a slow week, but you've overscheduled yourself. Whether you've taken on too much work, scheduled too many meetings, or said yes when you should have said no, we can all relate.

Sometimes you just have to get through an overscheduled and busy week. Even if your commitments are work obligations, be encouraged—you can still find peace.

Whenever you take a quick time-out to eat lunch, take a slow walk around the office, or drive to your next event, let your mind and body relax. Take long, deep breaths in between meetings. Let a few calls go to voice mail. Give thanks for your food, and take a few minutes to simply sit at lunch with no emails or texts. No, it probably won't feel as good as a two-hour nap or an afternoon at the spa, but these small moments will refresh your workday. Wherever and whenever you can take a minute, find peace in the moment.

....

I feel overwhelmed today, Lord. The to-do lists are endless, and my job responsibilities are full. Open up moments of refreshment, and help me use them well. Give me grace to push through, knowing that You are right there with me.

....
....
....
....
....
....
....
....
....
....
....
....
....
....
....
....
....
....
....

*After his suffering, [Jesus] presented himself to them and gave
many convincing proofs that he was alive. He appeared to them
over a period of forty days and spoke about the kingdom of God.*

Acts 1:3

If you watch the news for five minutes, listen to talk radio, or
glance at the headlines, you'll know our world is extremely broken.
Violence, war, injustice, racism, poverty, and more are all still very
much alive today—as well as quick fixes, insta-success, and moral
failures.

In the middle, it can feel overwhelming for a working mother.
How do you find stability for yourself and your family while manag-
ing a career and living in a messy world? Take heart; when the world
feels brutal and overwhelmingly broken, God is still working. When
the news makes your heart race, find courage, because God's love and
redemption will prevail in the end.

Today, life can seem challenging from every angle. But suffering
and compromise don't get the last word. The almighty God gets the
last word—and He promises rest, restoration, and healing. Cling to
that knowledge today, and rest in the enduring promises of a very loving God.

....

*When the world feels brutal and broken, may I see glimpses of Your love and
grace, Jesus. When moral failures and short-term solutions aren't enough,
let me find salvation in Your truth and mercy.*

Day 70

Out of his fullness we have all received grace
in the place of grace already given.

JOHN 1:16

You messed up. You lost your temper. You crossed the line. You chose evil over good. You got frustrated with a coworker. Can you relate to any of these statements?

As humans, we fall over and over again. We shake our heads at our mistakes, feel ashamed, beat ourselves up, and disappoint many. We fall into temptation's trap, act unjustly, and let sin rule our minds. But still, there is grace—grace upon grace upon grace—and the very real assurance of God's never-ending grace is like a deep well of water for a thirsty soul.

God knows we are sinners. He knows our shortcomings and struggles. He knows about that sin you just can't seem to break free from, and He offers you grace. It doesn't make sense, and it isn't contingent on anything you do. It's a reflection of God's goodness and mercy.

....

I don't deserve Your grace, yet You lavish it upon me over and over again. Thank You, Lord, for meeting me where I most need it—in the midst of my failures and mistakes.

....

....

....

....

....

....

....

....

....

....

....

....

....

....

....

....

....

....

....

....

"If my people, who are called by my name, will humble
themselves and pray and seek my face and turn from
their wicked ways, then I will hear from heaven, and
I will forgive their sin and will heal their land."

2 Chronicles 7:14

Have you ever done anything shameful? Are there sins you're embarrassed to tell even your closest confidant? Do you find yourself hiding from God because your failures are too shocking? Dear one, God can handle the truth.

He asks for obedience, but He welcomes the sinner. He knows no sin, but He loves those who are bound by it. God knows the darkest, most appalling parts of you, and if you confess them to Him, He will not turn you away. Instead, He will wash you clean.

If you're running from the Lord or trying to overwork or overperform, pause, take a deep breath, and turn to Him. You have a lot on your plate as a working mom. You are constantly running in several directions at once. Stop, and let Him in. Know that there is nothing you can do that is beyond His forgiveness. And there is no way He can love you more or love you less. God can handle the truth, and He longs for you to stop running and, instead, rest in His healing presence.

....

Here I am, Lord, broken and sinful. Thank You for loving me and covering
me at home, at work, and in all ways with Your grace. Deliver me of my
shame, and help me walk in Your light and mercy.

*The best-equipped army cannot save a king, nor
is great strength enough to save a warrior.*

PSALM 33:16 NLT

A strong work ethic is a great quality to have. It means you're a hard worker, productive, and reliable. But sometimes a strong work ethic can actually work against you. There's a problem when you begin working endless hours, skipping meals and breaks, and getting little sleep.

God calls us to work hard. He wants us to work to the best of our ability and to honor and glorify His name through our efforts. But He doesn't want to see us burned out, struggling to stay awake, and becoming resentful of our jobs.

Does your work ethic work against you? Admit that you can't do it all—because you weren't created to do it all. Don't forget the importance of rest. Take a Sabbath. Go on a weekend trip. Do something that you enjoy and that will help you refill your energy. God worked, and then He rested. Take some time to follow His example.

....

I admit that I can't do it all, Lord. Rescue me with Your rest. Please give me peace that passes my understanding so that I can walk in fullness with You.

As God's chosen people, holy and dearly loved, clothe yourselves
with compassion, kindness, humility, gentleness and patience.

COLOSSIANS 3:12

I f I am not there, everything will fall apart."

Many people feel this way about their responsibilities, whether they're a working mom, an executive assistant, the president of a non-profit, or a committed volunteer at the mission.

It's true, things may become a little chaotic if you aren't there. You are worth a lot. You might return to more work, a frazzled spouse, or a little disarray. But you might not. And either way, life will go on—even without you there to guide, lead, prod, and pick up the slack.

If you are holding out on rest because you think you're indispensable, you should reconsider. Give someone else a chance to step up, practice responsibility, and increase their confidence—and allow yourself time for peace. Take a step back and let things go for a day or even just a few hours. Life will go on, and you'll return feeling more equipped, capable, and energetic.

....

Lord, help me remember that the world won't fall apart if I take time away to find peace. You will provide, You always do, when I take refuge in You. I don't have to rule the world. I can let go and let You be King.

....

....

....

....

....

....

....

....

....

....

....

....

....

....

....

....

....

....

....

Commit your way to the LORD; trust in him and he will do this.

PSALM 37:5

We all crave balance as working moms, don't we? There's a societal obsession with finding the perfect balance of work, rest, family, hobbies, and friends. We want it all, but too often we're trapped in the misconception of needing to have it all and have it all right now. To put it mildly, finding balance is really hard—and we fail at it all the time.

When you feel as if you can't figure it out and the puzzle of balance just has too many pieces, turn to the Lord. He's the master Problem-Solver. He knows exactly what you need, and He knows how to help you achieve that elusive balance in your life.

Breathe easier, knowing that God is the ultimate Provider of peace, work, and community. He knows these are all good things, and He knows that you sometimes need help balancing them all. Ask God for help, and then wait patiently for His answer.

....

I'm so relieved, Lord, that You are the master Problem-Solver—and that it's not all up to me. Help me to remember Your Word, to hide it in my heart, and to believe You will fulfill it.

....

....

....

....

....

....

....

....

....

....

....

....

....

....

....

....

....

....

Restore us, LORD God Almighty; make your
face shine on us, that we may be saved.

PSALM 80:19

Whether you work in an office or are a college student while also being a mom, you probably have a long to-do list. And some tasks are more pressing than others. That deadline is crucial; your final exam is important; meeting the needs of hungry kids is a must. There are many priorities in your life, but how can you prioritize peace?

Anxiety likes to take its turn. You sacrifice sleep—and it's often for good things. You choose a date night over going to bed early. You prepare for a work presentation instead of sleeping in. You cuddle a sick baby and skip a nap of your own. But how often can you sacrifice rest before you are running ragged?

Today, try to prioritize rest in some way. Bump it closer to the top of your list. You'll feel more refreshed and positive, and those around you will benefit too.

Lord, I often push rest completely off my to-do list. Please show me opportunities today to restore my sense of peace, worth, and hope in You. Restore me to Your life and Your purpose.

Day 76

Then a great and powerful wind tore the mountains
apart and shattered the rocks before the LORD,
but the LORD was not in the wind.

I KINGS 19:11

Is your television always on or is your phone constantly begging for your attention? Do you numb your pain or shut down your thoughts by scrolling through your phone? Our worlds are often noisy, and even though it may feel uncomfortable, we need to seek out a distraction-free place in order to hear God.

When do you seek a break from the noise? Do you look for it in the early-morning hours when the moon is fading away, or is it in the evening when the stars are quietly shining? Maybe you protect a few minutes of your afternoon by setting a meeting on your agenda just for you, or you take time after your workday to walk and talk with the Lord.

There will always be noise and something vying for your attention. Be sure to intentionally set aside time to sit in the stillness and to listen for the still, small, and pure voice of God.

. . . .

God, I am often bombarded by the loud demands of this world. Sometimes, this is by my choosing. Remind me to make room and listen for Your still, small voice and to relish in Your care.

....

....

....

....

....

....

....

....

....

....

....

....

....

....

....

....

....

....

....

I pray that from his glorious, unlimited resources he will
empower you with inner strength through his Spirit.

EPHESIANS 3:16 NLT

Imagine yourself with a sweet child. But instead of treating that child with love and gentleness, you place high demands on her. You wake her after only a few hours of sleep, you make her scrub the floors without breakfast, and you allow her to eat only as you're rushing out the door. After school, you hand her an impossible to-do list—and when dinnertime comes and she hasn't completed it, you yell. You keep her up way past her bedtime and make her feel ashamed when she falls asleep on the couch. Who would treat a child that way?

But . . . is that the way you treat yourself?

Self-care is essential for living a healthy life, and it is also so easy to neglect. Treat yourself like a child today: God's child. Relax your expectations, be kind to yourself, and rest when you get overwhelmed. Care for yourself, even in your work.

....

Lord, help me tend to my own physical, spiritual, and emotional needs as
a loving parent tends to a child. Even though working is essential, peace is
also essential. Help me to bring balance to my life from the inside out.

....

....

....

....

....

....

....

....

....

....

....

....

....

....

....

....

....

....

....

Perfume and incense bring joy to the heart, and the
pleasantness of a friend springs from their heartfelt advice.

PROVERBS 27:9

L ean on Me," the song released in 1972, is a good reminder to all of us—we can lean on our friends when we're not strong; we need to give up our pride and ask for help; we all need someone to lean on.

How often do you lean on your friends? If you need to delegate responsibilities at work, do you assign tasks to a coworker? When you are behind on your big work project, do you ask your friends for prayers? If you need an hour to yourself, do you call a friend to watch your children?

Our friends help us carry on. They care for us and want to help us, whether it's with action, prayer, or simply a listening ear. When you're weary, call on a friend. Admit that you can't do everything on your own, and your friend will be there in a flash, saying, "Lean on me."

....

I praise You, Lord, for putting friends and coworkers in my life to lean on
when I'm in need. Remind me to express gratitude for all those who have
helped me in the past and those who are helping me now.

The eyes of the LORD are everywhere, keeping
watch on the wicked and the good.

PROVERBS 15:3

As you read this book, do you feel the urge to get up and do something? Start working, answer emails, or check your phone? Are you comfortable sitting still, or do you feel a bit of guilt about even taking time to read this?

We all need time to simply be still, so let yourself sit. God desires to speak to you, and He often speaks loudest when you push away distractions, stop working, and open your ears to what He has to say. Sitting still may feel lazy or unnatural. It may take everything you have not to scroll through your to-do list or check your inbox. But being in the Lord's presence may actually be the most productive part of your whole day.

Start your morning with the Giver of life. Let Him carry you and speak to you. Your mindset and attitude are changed in the presence of the Holy God—and all you need to do is be still and listen.

....

My ears are open, my body is still, and my spirit is ready. Speak to me,
precious Jesus. I am putting aside all distractions to hear from You.

....

....

....

....

....

....

....

....

....

....

....

....

....

....

....

....

....

....

....

....

I was young and now I am old, yet I have never seen the
righteous forsaken or their children begging bread.

PSALM 37:25

If you find yourself struggling to be content, it's not surprising. We are bombarded with messages that we don't have enough. Advertisers tell us the happiest people have the most prestigious job, latest phone, biggest wardrobe, and largest bank account. We are discontented creatures, and it all began with Adam and Eve.

When Satan appeared to Adam and Eve and said they could have even more—they could be like God—they wanted it. They saw one thing they didn't have, they set their sights on it, and they sinned. Discontentment prompted the first sin, and we sometimes feel as if it cannot be overcome. But take heart. God can bring contentment to your heart.

Are you tired of striving for more? Find peace for your soul by turning to the Lord. When you feel discontentedness creeping in, ask God to show you true fulfillment in Him. Even the best job, the newest hairstyle, or the applause of others can't take the place of being content in the heart of your Creator.

....

I think I know what I need, Lord, but You truly know what I need. Show me
Your fulfillment and peace. Help me receive all that You are so that I find
my joy and wholeness in You.

....

....

....

....

....

....

....

....

....

....

....

....

....

....

....

....

....

....

....

....

Whoever gives thought to the word will discover
good, and blessed is he who trusts in the LORD.

PROVERBS 16:20 ESV

If you have a close friend who lives a long distance away, you know how wonderful it is when you're together. You may have to board an airplane or train, rent a car, or take the bus, but reconnecting with a friend is worth it. You won't let anything get in the way of meeting with your friend.

When you're finally together, you soak up every single second. You don't spend time worrying about what's going on back home, you don't waste hours on social media, and you forget about your work obligations. You get to take time off from responsibility, and you simply get to be.

Your time with the Father can be the same. Even if you haven't connected with Him in a while, He is eagerly waiting for you, and He wants you to fiercely protect your time together with Him. Reconnect with the Lord today, and rejoice that He is always available and never far away.

....

Lord, I miss being close to You. Help me rest in Your compassionate embrace. Give me a desire to rest from work and take the time to connect with You. You are worthy of my time.

....

....

....

....

....

....

....

....

....

....

....

....

....

....

....

....

....

....

....

~~~~~~~~ *Day 82* ~~~~~~~~

Make it your ambition to lead a quiet life: You should mind your
own business and work with your hands, just as we told you.

I THESSALONIANS 4:11

*H*ave you noticed that while laundry detergent used to be limited to
a few different types, there are now hundreds of brands boasting
fresher scents, whiter whites, fewer chemicals, and more power? And
they come in liquids, powders, and pods. Have you ever stood in front
of a basic grocery item in the store—from crackers to shampoo—and
been utterly overwhelmed by the options?

In today's world, we love options. Whether we're searching for
cheap prices or products that are locally made, ethically sourced, or
organic, we can have our pick. But do you ever wish the options were
a bit more limited?

It may seem like a small, silly thing, but consider limiting your
options. Give yourself two options for dinner—tacos or spaghetti;
decide between two types of soap or three different selections of thank-
you cards. By reducing your choices, you'll save time, energy, and brain
space—and you'll open yourself up to peace.

....

Lord, teach me how to live more simply today. Whether it's at home, at
work, or in between, write minimalism on my heart. Show me the joy of Your
choices for me so that I can let go of unnecessary desires.

....

....

....

....

....

....

....

....

....

....

....

....

....

....

....

....

....

....

....

....

I said to myself, "Relax and rest. GOD has showered you with
blessings. Soul, you've been rescued from death; Eye, you've been
rescued from tears; and you, Foot, were kept from stumbling."
PSALM 116:7–8 MSG

Taking on a hobby is a great way to calm your mind. When your brain feels as if it's stuck in overdrive, and you've had a really long day at work, you should take a step back, take a break, and immerse yourself in a restful hobby.

Gardening, listening to music, baking, biking, and cooking are all rewarding stress relievers. Reading, fishing, writing, knitting, golfing, and hiking are a few more examples of mind-calming activities.

God created each of us with talents and interests outside of work activities, and we each can find hobbies we enjoy. If you're feeling stressed, turn to a relaxing hobby this week. You don't have to be great at it—the act of going fishing may be just as rewarding as actually catching a bass, and taking a bike ride can be more rejuvenating than participating in a race. The goal isn't to excel. The goal is to relax and enjoy yourself—even if you burn the brownies.

Thank You for making rest enjoyable, Lord. Remind me to take time to do
the things I love. When work is a lot to take in, show me ways to unwind
and remember the ways of fun.

....

....

....

....

....

....

....

....

....

....

....

....

....

....

....

....

....

....

I come to you for the shelter. Protect me, keep
me safe, and don't disappoint me.

PSALM 25:20 CEV

We have all experienced disappointment. In games, there's always a loser. In a job interview, only one person is hired. When a relationship fizzles, a dream is dashed, or another person gets what you so desperately wanted, disappointment can be incredibly painful and challenging. If we're not careful, disappointment can lead to despair, and despair only brings misery and discontent.

When you're disappointed, moving forward can be tough. Wallowing and moping are much easier. But if you linger in the muck of disappointment, you'll constantly be fighting to keep your head above the water—which is completely exhausting, especially when you have plenty of other things on your to-do list.

Be encouraged. The Lord knows how it feels to be disappointed, and He wants to free you from its chains. Because of His power and love, you don't need to be consumed by a broken dream. Instead, you can move on with His joy and hope as your guide. Flee from disappointment and run straight into His waiting arms.

....

When I am disappointed, Lord, remind me that Your hope never fails.
Your Word is always fulfilling of every dream, desire, and goal. You are my
dreams come true.

So the promise is received by faith. It is given as a free gift.

ROMANS 4:16 NLT

God's love cannot be earned. If you give up all your possessions, move to a developing country, and serve the most unlovable of people, you will not be given a greater portion of God's love. If you volunteer for every church need, pray for each of your coworkers daily, and spend your time constantly searching for God's approval, you still won't be able to earn it.

God's love for you isn't based on performance. It's not rooted in how beautiful or popular, smart or successful you are. Instead, His love for you is like the love a father has for his children. It is a love that is yours simply because you are you.

Of course, God is delighted when you serve the church, the needy, your colleagues, and the sick. He wants you to be more and more like Him, and He grieves when you sin. But regardless of your actions, His love does not waver, and it does not change. You can rest in that promise.

....

Father, remind me that in trying to earn Your love, I am doubting Your grace—and forgive me! In Your merciful truth, I ask to receive my worth from Your gift on the cross. Thank You for Your unconditional love.

"I will tend them in a good pasture, and the mountain heights of Israel will be their grazing land. There they will lie down in good grazing land, and there they will feed in a rich pasture on the mountains of Israel."

EZEKIEL 34:14

We can sleep when we're dead." Perhaps you've seen that phrase on billboards, social media, or even on a T-shirt. It's a funny saying—at least on the surface—but taken seriously, that mindset can lead you to exhaustion.

Approaching life in that way may seem ambitious and exciting. The world is your oyster, and there are so many things to see, taste, and experience. But, at the heart of it, that mindset undervalues peace. Overworking or spending your life traveling isn't necessarily going to serve you well. Rest is an important and healthy part of a balanced life. If you take time out to rest and rejuvenate, you're not missing out on life or the next job promotion.

Don't feel guilty if you can't do it all. You know your limits, and you know that in order to be a functioning, healthy person, you need peace. Don't succumb to the fear of missing out. Instead, rest in the Lord, and He'll bless you with an adventure-filled and successful life.

....

I praise You, Lord, for leading me to rest and restoring my soul. Remind me that I miss out on You when I believe the lie that You are not enough to fulfill my heart. You are always enough, and I can always find satisfaction in You.

....

....

....

....

....

....

....

....

....

....

....

....

....

....

....

....

....

....

....

....

Now, our God, we give you thanks, and

praise your glorious name.

I Chronicles 29:13

How often do you stop to count your blessings? It is easy, so very easy, to look at all that you don't have. But a life of constant wanting leads to a life of constant striving. Be encouraged to find contentment through thanksgiving today.

When you choose to focus on all that you do have, from the tiniest blessings to the biggest, your heart can't help but rejoice. A cool shower after an afternoon in the sun, a car that safely transports you to work, healthy children, food on the table—these are daily blessings.

Pause for a few minutes today and give thanks to the Lord, for He is good. All the good things in your life are His blessings to you—from the fragrant roses in your front yard to your coworker in the office space next to you. He is a good God who loves to give good gifts to His children. Rest in gratitude today.

....

For all Your blessings, love, and mercy, I thank You. Remind me to count my blessings, to gather joy, and to always give thanks for every circum-stance.

....

....

....

....

....

....

....

....

....

....

....

....

....

....

....

....

....

Then He arose and rebuked the wind, and said to the sea, "Peace,
be still!" And the wind ceased and there was a great calm.

MARK 4:39 NKJV

The forecast for your life may look bleak. You can see that there is pain, stress, suffering, or turmoil ahead. Your shoulders begin to hunch against the burden, and your heart races in fear. You're just not sure if you're strong enough for a storm this big.

When you see storm clouds rolling into your life, you may feel completely beaten. You might feel angry, sad, confused, or afraid. And you may even wonder how in the world you'll get through it all. Here is your answer—take refuge in the Lord.

Your Father in heaven might not stop the storm from coming. But He will walk through it with you. So even if the circumstances around you look treacherous, you can tell your heart, "Peace, be still!"—because Jesus is with you in the boat of life. Settle into His protective arms, and rest knowing that He provides respite and refuge.

....

You are my Rock, my Peace, and my Refuge, Jesus. Thank You for Your
strength in my life, especially when I don't know what to do. Help me with
my fear.

....

....

....

....

....

....

....

....

....

....

....

....

....

....

....

....

....

....

....

For the foolishness of God is wiser than human wisdom, and
the weakness of God is stronger than human strength.

I Corinthians 1:25

I want to be a better parent. I want to have a better job. I want to get better grades. I want to be a more loving friend.

There are so many ways we can better ourselves, and as Christians, we should try to be the best we can be. We each need to do our best to be a good mother, neighbor, friend, sister, colleague, or boss. And yes, we need to do all things as if we're doing them for God. But we also should acknowledge this truth: we can't be the best at everything.

Do you ever feel overwhelmed by everything you want—or feel you need—to excel at? Bring these concerns to the Lord. He knows exactly what you need, and He is able to help you see what is truly important. And He can gently, patiently, and tenderly transform you into the best version of yourself. Find rest by trusting in Him.

I want to be transformed, Lord, but I need Your grace to do it. Help me in my weakness, speak truth to me in my sin, and guide me with Your hand.

....
....
....
....
....
....
....
....
....
....
....
....
....
....
....
....
....
....
....
....

~~~~~~~~ *Day* 90 ~~~~~~~~

May the Lord direct your hearts into God's
love and Christ's perseverance.

2 THESSALONIANS 3:5

magine you have an early morning breakfast meeting. You wake to
your alarm, get dressed, and head out with visions of strong black
coffee. When you sit down at the table, a cup of steaming coffee is
placed in front of you. You take a sip. It's good.

The meeting begins, and your cup is half full. The waiter asks if
you'd like a refill but then adds only hot water to your cup. In fact, each
time he refills your cup, he adds only water, not coffee. Soon, the coffee
is only a memory floating in a cup of light-brown water. And you're left
feeling frustrated and cheated.

The same thing can happen with rest. You may begin your workweek strong and ready to take on the world. But if you make only
half-hearted attempts to maintain peace, you're going to feel watered
down by the end of the week with nothing to give your family. Make
it a point to refill your cup with peace this week.

....

Lord, remind me to refill with Your Word—and with You—instead of
watered-down substitutes. Be my Guide, my Fullness, and my Joy. I want
to serve others from an overflowing cup.

But as for me, I watch in hope for the Lord, I wait
for God my Savior; my God will hear me.

MICAH 7:7

*H*ave you ever wondered, *How did I end up here?* Life just doesn't look the way you envisioned it when you were younger. It's much harder—more responsibility, sorrow, pain, and stress. Playing house as a child doesn't compare to everyday life as an adult, does it?

When life isn't going the way you'd hoped, it's easy to be discouraged. Maybe you're working a dead-end job, or your dream of being a musician is fading. Your mom died too soon, your spouse left, parenthood is a tough battle, or your close friend betrayed you. Life throws curveballs, and sometimes you get hit.

How do you cope? How can you find peace and contentment? Scripture tells us that our only hope comes from God. Tell Him your struggles, and confide your fears in His ear. He is listening—and waiting to give you rest.

....

My hope, satisfaction, joy, and future are in You, my God, my Savior, and my King. Help me to find peace in You, whether in life, work, or family life. Teach me the ways of peace, and be the desire of my heart.

....

....

....

....

....

....

....

....

....

....

....

....

....

....

....

....

....

....

....

....

....

❋❋❋❋❋❋ Day 92 *❊❊❊❊❊❊*

For the sake of my family and friends, I
will say, "Peace be within you."
Psalm 122:8

When Jesus drew away from the crowds and found a place alone to pray, He was resting with His Father. He did it on purpose and with intention. How often do you find yourself resting intentionally and on purpose? And no, falling asleep on the couch doesn't count! Only intentional rest brings true restoration.

You have permission to intentionally let go today, friend. Sit with a cup of coffee for a few extra minutes. Take some time for an afternoon stroll through the park. Leave work an hour early, and enjoy some quality time with your spouse.

Continual work will leave you worn out and empty, but purposefully seeking out balance will bless you with restoration and renewal for your soul.

....

Restore my soul and renew my body, Father. Please draw near to me as I
intentionally place my trust in You. Thank You for the time to be heard and
healed.

....
....
....
....
....
....
....
....
....
....
....
....
....
....
....
....
....
....
....
....
....

"So do not fear, for I am with you; do not be dismayed,
for I am your God. I will strengthen you and help you;
I will uphold you with my righteous right hand."

ISAIAH 41:10

G od gives us big promises in the Bible. He promises never to leave or forsake us. He promises redemption and restoration to those who follow Him. And He promises that He has great plans and big dreams for us—greater than we could ever imagine. He declares that we are His masterpieces.

All of the Lord's promises are so good and so true, yet we live as though He's lying sometimes. We can live frantically—striving and struggling to achieve our work goals, prove ourselves, and attain approval as well. We often can say yes to too many things and no to too few for fear that others will be disappointed. Simply put, working moms can have a hard time resting in God's promises.

The Lord tells us not to worry or be anxious; He'll provide for our every need as we trust in Him. He tells us He delights in us, for we are His daughters. How miraculous! How graceful! Rest in the enduring, eternal, and perfect promises of God today.

....

Teach me to release my burdens to You. Teach me to delight in Your love for me, Father. Let me live a life that is loved, just as You have paid the price for.

May our Lord Jesus Christ himself and God our
Father . . . encourage your hearts and strengthen
you in every good deed and word.

2 THESSALONIANS 2:16–17

When the sun sets and you fall into bed after a particularly rough day, do you ever feel as if the whole world is against you? Your kids are demanding, your work is stressing you out, your responsibilities are overwhelming, and everything would be so much better if you just had a little more time. Sound familiar?

Rest assured, after every bad night there is a new sunrise, every frustrating day can be followed by a joyful evening, and each bad start can end with a fantastic finish. When God says His mercies are new every morning, He means it. He has more than enough grace for you each day. You can be sure of it—as sure as the sun rises. Find peace today knowing that God gives you new beginnings . . . over and over and over again.

....

Thank You, Jesus, for Your grace upon grace—every morning, evening, and moment in between. Great is Your faithfulness.

A person's wisdom yields patience; it is to
one's glory to overlook an offense.

PROVERBS 19:11

*H*urry up! What's taking you so long? I'm waiting on you again."
Have you often found yourself saying these things? Perhaps you
directed them at a colleague or a spouse or a child. Or perhaps you even
shouted these things at God when He was slow to reveal an answer.

While some people are naturally patient, most of us have to work
at it again and again. But over time and through prayer, you can calm
your impatient heart and find a deep well of patience. Cultivating
patience will allow you to wait instead of act, ask instead of demand,
and trust the Lord's plan instead of forging ahead with your own.
Patience means that when things don't happen exactly according to
your schedule, you're able to handle it gracefully. Choosing patience
instead of impatience will reward you with rest and peace. No, it won't
always be easy, but it will always be worth it.

Father, please change my impatience to patience, my skepticism to trust,
my frustration to peace. Help me to wait for You with deep assurance.

....
....
....
....
....
....
....
....
....
....
....
....
....
....
....
....
....
....
....
....

*Who compares with you among gods, O GOD? Who
compares with you in power, in holy majesty, in
awesome praises, wonder-working God?*

EXODUS 15:11 MSG

Children are the best at enjoying the small things—a solitary bubble, a caterpillar, a balloon, a ride on the lawn mower, a dandelion. It doesn't matter if it's a tiny puddle or a huge swimming pool, a trip to the shoe store or to Disney World: kids are able to see the smallest of moments and things as opportunities for wonder and joy.

When did we lose that? When did we become so hard to impress and so difficult to captivate? Every day we rush past so many tiny but great moments simply because we're too busy or too distracted.

Give yourself permission to slow down today. Let your gaze linger over the sunrise, savor that delicious lunch with all your senses, and be on the lookout for the amazing and beautiful. God has placed it all around you, even if it's a workday. Open your eyes, and rest in its wonder.

....

*Lord, help me slow down, refocus, and be on the lookout for Your wonders
all around me. Even when I'm at the office, open my eyes to the beauty and
joy of the day.*

....

....

....

....

....

....

....

....

....

....

....

....

....

....

....

....

....

....

....

....

....

....

You will keep in perfect peace those whose minds
are steadfast, because they trust in you.
ISAIAH 26:3

Your body and mind cry, *Go to bed*, but you refuse because there are still half a dozen things to finish up for the day. Have you experienced that lately?

While some tasks must be finished (a work project, feeding the baby, paying a bill), there are many other responsibilities that can be put off for another time.

If you feel exhausted, ask yourself, *Are there negative consequences for not finishing this today?* Then weigh the pros and cons. Sometimes you may just have to push through and finish up. But often, it's simply our pride or stubbornness that stands between us and peace.

Even if things aren't finished, if the house is a mess and the dishes are piled in the sink, even if you aren't done with all those work emails, peace is more important. Let yourself off the hook a bit and allow yourself to find balance even if a few things must remain undone.

....

I want to make peace my priority, Lord. Help me trust that everything else will fall into place when I give You all the pieces of my day. Remind me to seek the kingdom first.

....

....

....

....

....

....

....

....

....

....

....

....

....

....

....

....

....

....

....

....

The Lord looks down from heaven on all mankind to see
if there are any who are wise, who want to please God.

PSALM 14:2 TLB

I'm disappointed in you. I was counting on you. I needed you, and *you weren't there.* Those are hard words to hear. Some people so dread disappointing others that they strive to please everyone all the time. They work hard to make sure everyone is happy.

But trying to please everyone is exhausting and impossible. Admit it, you can't make everyone happy. Of course, you can say yes to some things, but it's not your duty to say yes to everything. Sometimes you simply need to say no to others and yes to God and yourself. Putting God first and giving some priority to nourishing your own body and soul are actually key components in being able to serve others well.

Do you need to put a pause on pleasing others today? Ask the Lord to help you put pleasing Him at the top of your to-do list.

....

Jesus, help me establish healthy boundaries and remind me to focus on You first and foremost. It's not selfish to care for myself, and I need Your strength to be confident in that.

....

....

....

....

....

....

....

....

....

....

....

....

....

....

....

....

....

....

Therefore, since we are surrounded by such a great
cloud of witnesses, let us throw off everything that
hinders and the sin that so easily entangles. And let us
run with perseverance the race marked out for us.

HEBREWS 12:1

You wanted to finish that big project at work, vacuum your home, take the car to the shop, check in with your loved one, cook dinner, and get ahead on your Bible study. But none of those things happened, and you're left feeling really discouraged. We've all had those sorts of days.

Sometimes you may need to adjust your expectations. They may simply be too high, and you run the risk of getting stuck in a vicious cycle of unmet expectations and disappointment. It's okay, at times, to throw your hands up and say, "I'll try again tomorrow."

Is it time to ease up on your expectations a little? Would it really be disastrous if you didn't finish everything today? God promises to always take care of you—and that promise doesn't end if your to-do list isn't finished. Let go of your expectations today, and instead, ask God to help you look at your day through the lens of His expectations.

....

God, help me adjust my expectations and live according to Your plans, not my own. I am not the savior of the world, You are. Thank You for giving me life.

....
....
....
....
....
....
....
....
....
....
....
....
....
....
....
....
....
....

God did not send his Son into the world to condemn
the world, but to save the world through him.

JOHN 3:17

When your perspective shifts to an eternal viewpoint, suddenly a lot of once-important things fall to the wayside. In light of eternity, many of our daily stressors or worries simply become insignificant.

Of course, it's all too easy to get caught up in your children's extracurricular activities. It's common to be ultra-focused on your résumé, making sure it will dazzle any prospective employer. Your job helps pay the bills, and you want to ensure job security, so you work all hours of the day and night. Life is busy, and there are lots of important matters pulling you in every direction. Many of them are good. But, in light of eternity, they aren't necessarily life-and-death concerns.

If you find yourself consumed by busyness, frazzled and frantic in getting everything done, look to the Lord. Ask Him to clear your vision and your mind. And try to look at your day with an eternal perspective.

....

God, remind me that this life is simply a blip in time, and eternity is what truly matters. When I get focused on earthly things, show me the delight of living with a kingdom mindset.

Notes

1. Kelli Catana, "The Average Working Mom Works 98 Hours a Week," Moms.com, January 19, 2019, https://www.moms.com/working-mom-works-98-hours/.